The Taste of Anger

The Taste of Anger

A Memoir

Diane Vonglis Parnell

SHE WRITES PRESS

Published 2024
Printed in the United States of America
Print ISBN: 978-1-64742-684-2
E-ISBN: 978-1-64742-685-9
Library of Congress Control Number: 2024901708

For information, address:
She Writes Press
1569 Solano Ave #546
Berkeley, CA 94707

Interior Design by Tabitha Lahr

She Writes Press is a division of SparkPoint Studio, LLC.

Excerpts of memoir published by Fish Publishing; Blame the Milkman, Fish Anthology, 2022

A percentage of the profits from sales of this book will be donated to CASA SLO (slocasa.org), a non-profit organization dedicated to helping abused and neglected children in our local court system.

For Dean and Conor

> *"The whole world into which I was born had become an unbearable burden, and I wished I could reduce it to some small thing that I could hold underwater until it died."*

—JAMAICA KINCAID, *ANNIE JOHN*

Contents

Prologue

"I'll kill the first person who comes through this doorway! I swear I will!"

I freeze when I hear shouting coming from the house. It's my father's voice—not my brothers, Matt and Michael, who had gone in thinking it was empty, thinking it was safe. I watch as my father backs them off the porch and onto the sidewalk, a baseball bat gripped in his meaty hands, up in the air, over his right shoulder.

Matt takes another step backward at the warning.

Michael holds his ground. "Calm down. We're just here to get some of our stuff."

I stand in the driveway at the bottom of the hill beside my mother and my other six siblings, my heart thumping against my ribs. This was not the plan we had gone over earlier in the day: show up at the farm when we knew my father wouldn't be there, get in and out before he came back. We had boxes to collect clothing, sheets and pillows, and a few pots and pans. That had been the plan when we pulled into the driveway. But he had tricked us, hiding his truck somewhere, and then ambushed my brothers at the door.

"Rose," he yells at my mother, "get your boys out of here." He holds the bat higher, standing wide-legged in the porch doorway. Teeth bared, face purple. "I'll kill 'em. I swear. I'll kill 'em."

"Mom, I think we better go," Lizzy whispers. "He'll do it. You know he'll do it."

I read my mother's ashen face. The bewildered blinking as she, too, processes the scene: *He wasn't supposed to be here.* She looks at Lizzy, then at the rest of us. I hold my breath, waiting for her to move.

"Okay, boys," she finally calls to my brothers. "Let's go."

Matt and Michael tromp through the snow and back down the hill, never taking their eyes off my father as they get behind the wheels of the borrowed trucks.

"Everybody get back in the car." My mother hurries to the front of our old station wagon and drops into the driver's seat. Lizzy slides into the passenger side. Luke, Mary, and I get in behind her as my three youngest brothers clamber into the way-back seat.

I watch my mother's hand shake as she struggles to get the key in the ignition. I want to scream at her—*Hurry! Hurry! Get us out of here!*—before my father flies off the porch and rushes down the driveway, smashing the car windows with the bat and then dragging us out, one at a time, to beat us to death.

Finally, the engine starts, and my mother quickly backs the wagon down the driveway. I can only exhale when our procession is far, far up the road.

It is December 27, 1974. I am fifteen years old.

1962

Blame the Milkman

We descend like fleas, tumbling out of our battered blue-and-white Chevy onto a dirt driveway slippery with patches of snow and ice. All nine of us, decked out in our Sunday best, freshly blessed from church. My father, in his black suit and narrow necktie, lines us up and reminds us to behave when we go inside. The wind snaps my mother's floral dress around her shins as she straightens collars and combs hair while cradling the baby in the crook of her arm.

I take in the barren landscape as I wait my turn for the comb's scrutiny. Field after flat field dusted with snow, separated by hedgerows of naked spindly trees and sagging wire fences. A half-mile to the north, at the top of the hill, I spy a house, the only one we passed on the long gravel road leading here. From this distance, it is a tiny brick-red smear on the horizon.

I turn my attention to the farmhouse, which is hunched under the muddy sky like a wet dog. Its ancient, brittle shingle siding is brown, and the windows hold rectangles of yellow-filmed glass. Across the yard, a small wooden structure leans left atop a pile of cinderblocks. I watch my sister Kathy's skeptical eye appraise the place as she lifts Luke to her hip. The sniff she makes tells me exactly how she feels about this ramshackle property out here in East Avon, or what she calls *the boondocks*. Kathy is the oldest, at seven, followed by Matt, Lizzy, Michael, me, Luke, and Mary, the baby.

Lizzy clamps my hand in hers as we fall in behind my father, who takes the lead, cutting a trail through the dirty snow and piles of debris littering the yard. An old woman, bird-thin with white cropped hair, greets us at a porch door that squeaks open on rusted hinges.

"Come in, come in!" she shouts. "I'm Betty, Betty Hawkins." She extends her hand to my father, staring openly at the bunch of us. My brothers in their white shirts and ties, hair slicked back in Brylcreem swooshes. My sisters and I are in dresses tight under the armpits, our hair curled.

"My, so many children," she exclaims, shaking her head.

This is something we hear a lot. Each time, my father puffs up like a peacock in full-feather regalia, as he does now, presenting us to the old woman one at a time, like gifts.

Safely hidden in the crowd until my turn, I look around the cluttered, chaotic mess of the porch. Large, wooden crates strewn about the floor overflow with rusted tools, broken kerosene lanterns, and greasy automobile parts. Crooked shelves hold mason jars packed with thick, liquid mysteries and tin cans full of nuts and bolts.

We follow Mrs. Hawkins up a step and through a doorway into a small room with a low ceiling and a single window. The plaster in the walls is thin and crumbling in many places, exposing rows of lath that stick out like ribs. Jackets, overalls, and hats hang on hooks above mud-caked boots. In the far-right corner, a claw-foot tub sits inside a doorless and otherwise empty room. My mother peers in, turning to Mrs. Hawkins, and asks where the sink and toilet are. The old woman laughs, pulling my mother by the elbow over to the window.

"Didn't you see the outhouse on your way in?" She points at the left-leaning building in the middle of the yard. "The sink is in the kitchen."

"Oh," my mother says.

The house itself is dark, late-night dark, and smells of old newspapers. Mrs. Hawkins leads us past a room cluttered with heavy furniture and dusty boxes, then through a kitchen so narrow we have to walk single file. A doorway beyond reveals a room with sooty walls and a potbelly stove coughing smoke into the air.

Mr. Hawkins hoists himself out of a worn, overstuffed chair and ambles over to my father, pumping his hand up and down in welcome. He is round in a Humpty Dumpty kind of way with brown trousers that look scratchy.

"Sit, sit," he says in a soft, slow drawl. My father takes a chair while Mom eases herself onto the couch, lifting Mary to her shoulder. The rest of us scatter silently around the room to sit on the filthy, wood floor.

The men do most of the talking, both waving hands of dismissal at my mother when she asks about indoor plumbing. Mr. Hawkins gets up and throws a shovelful of coal into the stove, making the fire inside roar to life like a sleeping dragon that has just had its tail stepped on.

"Did I mention the outhouse is a double-seater?" He eyes my parents over his glasses as he settles back into his chair with a satisfied *harrumph.*

He and my father iron out the details of the sale: the house, the barns, the farm equipment, and the forty-eight acres that are all part of the property at 2727 Swamp Road. They seal the deal with another handshake.

It's the milkman's fault we are leaving our city home in Rochester, and moving to this farm. He and his high milk prices are to blame for what my father calls "our financial woes." Lately, my father has been drumming his fingers on the kitchen table a lot before heading off to his factory job at Gleason Works, complaining about how he's sick of the milkman stealing his hard-earned money.

"I'm gonna buy a farm, get a cow, and then have all the milk I want for free," he declared months before buying the farmhouse. My mother laughed the first time he brought this plan up, saying neither one of them knew a thing about farming.

"We'll learn," my father asserted. When she realized he was serious, she resisted, arguing that it was comfortable in the city, that we had a good school, good neighbors, and friends nearby. But he argued back, saying we would find another good school, and neighbors, and friends. The topic came up for days, and each time, my mother got quieter and quieter.

We sleep on the bare wooden floor during our first night in our new home because my father is too tired to put the beds together. I lay awake long after the others, grateful for his snoring, which punctures the quiet and absolute blackness of the farmhouse. Even though all nine of us are packed together in this one room, I feel lonely. Not alone, just lonely. It is a new sensation, heavy in my stomach and cold like the planked floor beneath me.

I wake in the night, aware of my mother sitting against a wall in the darkness, nursing Mary. I want to tiptoe between my slumbering siblings and sit beside her to whisper in her ear all that I am feeling. I want the warmth of her body next to mine. But Mom has been crabby a lot while packing for this move, and if I accidentally wake anyone on my way over to her, I know she will scold me and send me straight back to my spot on the floor.

A war is on in our new home from the moment we arrive—my mother battling against the rats that prowl the house at night in search of food. She finds a fat one on the kitchen table in the morning, eating its way through a loaf of Wonder Bread. We gather around her, staring bug-eyed at the shredded white plastic bag it left behind.

Each night, my mother smears peanut butter onto big wooden traps and slides them into cupboards and under the kitchen sink. I awake in the dark to the *snap* of a trap from below, and then the sound of critters scampering through the walls. *Dalump dalump dalump*—it is more of a stampede than the pitter-patter of a lone rodent on the run.

In the mornings, if Mom hasn't yet emptied the traps, we find rats pinned to them, heads crushed by the metal spring, dried blood around their noses. Or worse, a rat that is still alive, squirming and squealing a high-pitched sound that goes right through my head. I watch Mom lift the flat shovel she keeps against the kitchen wall just for this purpose, whacking the thing over and over until it lies still. Seeing my mother in her new role as rat killer unsettles me.

There is a large hole in the kitchen wall, close to the floor that Mom plugs with a dishrag, but the rats pull it away. Sometimes, while we eat breakfast, one will poke its head out of the hole, scaring the bejesus out of my siblings and me as we scream and lift our feet in case it runs out. Mom tries to make us laugh by shaking her finger at the hole and saying in a funny voice, "I'm gonna get you, Mr. Rat. You just wait." We watch the whiskered snout disappear as she thrusts a broom handle through the hole.

This makes me feel a little better about the rats during the day, but then night comes with the *snap* of the traps and rats fleeing through the walls. In the attic bedroom I share with my four older siblings, I lie in the dark, heart pounding, worried a rat will find a hole like the one in the kitchen wall, climb through it, and jump onto my bed to bite me in the face.

Every sound in this old farmhouse is amplified in the night's ebony stillness, and as the others sleep in their bunk beds around me, I lay blinking and listening to distant creaks and whines. I miss the old bedroom I shared with just two of my sisters, and my old house where there were no rat traps going off all night. I miss the familiar sound of cars passing in front of the house, their headlights illuminating my bedroom ceiling, and the sense of safety I felt from the close walls of the neighbors' houses. I might never sleep if not for being hypnotized by the nightly syncopated chorus of crickets, which eventually lulls me back into slumber.

Daylight is better than nighttime, but not by much. Everything is foreign in this new place, like the outhouse in the yard. On day one, my older siblings and I stumble through the tall weeds toward the little shack, following my father for our first lesson in outhouse use. He climbs the steps, ducking as he passes through the doorway, and beckons us in.

A dank, out-of-the-ground smell permeates the air, and in the dim light, I search in vain for a switch on the cobwebby walls. I expect a white toilet like at our old house, with a fuzzy blue elastic rug wrapped around the lid, a flusher, and an extra roll of toilet paper on the tank. Instead, the space is filled with a long, rough-hewn plywood box running along the back wall and round wooden lids covering side-by-side holes on top. The double-seater Mr. Hawkins promised.

We bunch together in the narrow space as my father lifts the lids and exposes the holes, slivery and misshapen. An eye-burning stench rises from within, along with a muffled buzzing sound I mistake for a swarm of angry bees. I step closer to Kathy, grab her hand, and press myself between her and Lizzy as several fat-bodied insects spiral up and out of the holes, diving and circling in the dusty air before landing on the walls.

"Just flies," Lizzy whispers down to me. I relax my grasp on Kathy's hand even though the buzzing continues deep inside the box.

After a lot of hesitation and you-go-firsts, my brothers and sisters follow my father's instructions, taking turns sitting over the holes, placing one hand firmly on the box to avoid falling in as they practice wiping with the other hand. I am too small to manage on my own, and when my father holds me up, I cling to him, legs wrapped around his waist, fearful I might plunge down the cavernous hole and be eaten alive by whatever is down there stinking and swarming. He shines a flashlight into the hole, and in the bright beam, I watch flies—dozens of them—flitting on the mounds of poop, soggy toilet paper, and crushed cardboard rollers.

Summer storms bring a week of rain, trapping us in the house, breathing down each other's necks. It doesn't take long for the fighting to begin. I stay clear of the ruckus, standing with my back against the wall as I watch my older siblings push and shove each other, arguing over toys and space. Michael is especially vicious, pounding his brother on the back when snatching a Tonka truck from Matt's hands. Matt is older, but his timidity is no match for Michael's aggression, and when Kathy is unable to pull them apart, Lizzy runs to Mom for help.

"For crying out loud! Would you keep your gol' darn hands off each other?" Mom, framed in the doorway with her hands on her hips, is as tired of us as we are of each other.

This constant chaos in our new house makes me uneasy. The living room is crammed with furniture—the couch, the TV, my father's chair and footstool, end tables, and a playpen—which leaves little floor space to play on. We had a playroom in our city house, so when Mom thought we were too loud, she just closed the door. Here, there is no playroom, and there are no doors on any of the rooms. Even my parents' bedroom (they sleep in the room with the potbelly stove) has only a heavy floral curtain draped over a pole to separate it from the kitchen. Their room is also cluttered with dressers along one wall, cribs for Luke and Mary, and a cedar chest at the foot of their bed.

While Mom scolds my siblings, I sneak away to the outhouse. Kathy used to help me in here, holding me in place while I went, but I learned how to balance on one arm like the rest of them do. I come out alone now, grateful to get away from the noise and tension in the house, grateful for some privacy, some peace and quiet. I secure the door latch, ignoring the flies, the stench, and the furry spiders in their corner webs, and climb onto the wooden box between the two holes. I lean my back against the wall, tuck my feet underneath me, and sit there puzzling over the events taking place in my new world.

It isn't just the fighting I want to get away from. The thing is, I just don't *like* it here in this old farmhouse. Both of my parents are always grouchy—Mom because she doesn't have the plumbing she says she needs, and my father because it takes him a lot longer to get to his job in the city.

I miss Mr. and Mrs. Saunders, the old couple from next door who came over in the mornings, scooping us into their warm laps while they drank coffee with Mom. I even miss our milkman, even though it's his fault we're here. I miss his crisp uniform and the shiny-billed hat that made him look like a police officer. And how we'd open the little door inside the house and say hello as he slid bottles into the milk chute. I'd stand on a chair to get a better look, fascinated by how his broad face filled the entire opening of the milk chute, like a giant peering into a tiny home. I miss the neighborhood kids playing on our swing set and how Mom would put a dollar in Kathy's hand to go down to the corner store to get candy for everyone. All we have here is each other, and without other kids around to give us a break, we get sick of our own company, making us moody and short-tempered.

A loud *bang, bang, bang* on the door shatters my thoughts and the silence. The door latch rattles; Lizzy pleads from outside. "Hurry up in there. I've gotta go *baaad*."

———————

Mom claims victory over the rats and removes all but one trap. *A just-in-case trap*, she says, loading it with peanut butter and sliding it under the sink. With the threat of the rats gone, mice appear in the house. Lizzy thinks they are cute, but Mom says *they're not cute, they're a nuisance*, and she sets small traps for them, ignoring Lizzy's long face.

Fall arrives and the crickets disappear, leaving the night world still and soundless. Without the constant interruption of rat traps springing shut, I sleep better, unafraid, and undisturbed by the occasional soft scratch of a mouse in the wall.

There is a new sound in the kitchen, though—a choking, guttural sound that penetrates the attic floorboards and startles me awake early one morning. I sit upright in bed to listen, my puzzlement turning to alarm when I realize it is my mother making these sounds. Frightened, I jump from my bed and shake Kathy awake.

"Something's wrong with Mom downstairs," I whisper, hunched close to her ear, my heart racing. Confusion crosses my sister's freckled face as her eyes flutter open. And then she, too, is listening. Rising up on her elbow, Kathy cocks her head as the sounds continue: gagging, coughing sounds. I hold my breath, waiting for her to react. Her eyes narrow, mouth turned down at the corners, and she collapses back onto her bed with a loud groan, pulling her pillow over her head, shutting me and my fear out.

I poke her arm again, hopping now from one foot to the other.

"Kathy, please," I beg in a voice loud enough to stir Lizzy, who peers down from her top bunk, eyes sleepy beneath dark bangs. Her face shows no hint of concern for the sounds below.

Kathy removes the pillow from her head with an exasperated sigh, and when she looks up at Lizzy, I am aware of something passing between them, like a secret in a sealed envelope.

"What's wrong with Mom?" I persist. "Shouldn't we go help her?"

"Don't worry, Mom's fine." Kathy is still looking at Lizzy. "She gets sick like this when she has a baby in her belly."

I frown, looking from one to the other, waiting for the smile at the joke they are trying to play on me.

"A baby in her belly? She can't have a baby in her belly. Mary's her baby."

"Well, she's going to have another one." Kathy shrugs.

I don't believe her. I say I want to go see for myself.

"No, don't go down there yet." Kathy shakes her head. "Wait until she's done."

The awful sounds stop, and I return to my bed, feigning sleep when Mom climbs the stairs and shuffles across the room telling Kathy, Matt, and Lizzy it's time to get up for school, acting like nothing just happened downstairs. I peer at her through the slits of my nearly-closed eyes. Her hair is in pin curls beneath a bandanna, her face pale and eyes watery, her frayed housecoat tied loosely around her large body. I want my mother to say something, or my sisters to say something, to acknowledge this news. But they hold their tongues, so I hold mine.

The sound of my mother's morning sickness wakes me again the next day, and the day after that. I stay put as Kathy had instructed, listening to her, but by the third morning, I cannot stand it any longer. I want to be with my mother, to console her, and so I tiptoe down the stairs, padding barefoot through the living room, toward the kitchen.

In the open doorway, I see my mother leaning over the sink, fingers gripping the edge of the counter. Her face is purple, eyes shut as vomit shoots from her mouth. She is gasping for air, gagging and vomiting again and again. Thoughts of comforting her disappear—what I am seeing is too scary, and I stand helpless in the doorway, wishing I had not come down after all. Wishing I had listened to Kathy.

I watch my mother's mouth open and close, fishlike, as the vomiting ends and dry retching ripples through her body. When it is finally over, she pulls a wadded handkerchief from her robe pocket and dabs at her mouth, elbows resting on the lip of the sink. Only then does she open her eyes and notice me there. Head still bowed toward the sink, she pockets the hanky and turns her swollen face in my direction.

"What are you doing up already?" Her words are hoarse and whispery. I can't think of a response, so I go to her, taking one of her robe's ties into my hand, wanting to be close but unable to look up at her. I want my mother to touch me with reassurance, to chase away the unease racing around inside of me. I want to feel the warmth of the palm of her hand on my head.

She reaches for the faucet, rinses away the vomit, then gently pulls away from me, moving down the counter to fill the percolator with water and spoon heaps of Maxwell House coffee into it. Her color has returned to normal, her breathing calmer.

"Go on back upstairs now and get dressed." She shoos me out of the room, scuffs over to the table, and lowers herself into a chair. "And tell the other kids it's time to get up for school."

I leave the kitchen, but instead of going upstairs, I hide behind my father's chair in the living room and watch my mother. The percolator bloops and hisses, and when it's done, she rises to fill her cup. Back at the table, she stares at the wall, stirs her coffee, stares at the wall some more. In the stillness, I wonder what she's thinking about. The kitchen clock ticks and tocks. She blows on her coffee. Takes a sip.

I don't leave my hiding spot until Mary begins crying from her crib. Mom stands to get her, and I scamper up the stairs on all fours, quieter than the mice in the walls.

1963

The Monster in the Barn

"Hallelujah for that!" My mother's hands rest on her swollen belly as the entire family gathers around the new toilet, entranced as though the flusher that swirls the water in the bowl and sends it disappearing down the hole is some sort of miracle, or something we've never seen before. The sight *is* something to behold, given how we've been using the outhouse for over a year now, tromping through snowdrifts in our boots, me with my nightgown hitched up, staying close to the bobbing beam of the flashlight in Kathy's hand because I'm afraid of the dark.

Grampa Murray, my mother's father, is here as well. He is actually the hero behind this miracle, coming here to show my father how to install the toilet, sink, and new bathtub. Grampa catches my eye and winks as he lights his pipe. I blush, smiling back, and when he sticks his index finger in his cheek to indicate my dimples, I blush even deeper. He takes a few satisfied puffs from his pipe, and then the whole room smells like Grampa.

"You got a door to put on this?" He turns to my father, rapping his knuckles on the bathroom doorframe.

"Not yet." My father shrugs. "I'll get one next week."

Mom wraps the toilet seat in the blue fuzzy cover from our old house, shooing us out of the room as she lays the matching rugs on the newly-tiled floor. Grampa packs up his tools and backs his truck out of the driveway. I hate to see him go and wave frantically from the window.

A month passes, and still my father hasn't put a door on the bathroom. Tired of asking, Mom puts a pole up and hangs another floral curtain in the doorway.

Upstairs at night, Kathy explains why it is important that this new baby be a boy.

"We're a girl-boy-girl-boy family so far." She ticks off our names: Kathy, Matt, Lizzy, Michael, Diane, Luke, Mary. "Get it?"

Captivated by this realization, my siblings and I nod with enthusiasm, propped up on our elbows in the bunk beds. During the day, we nag Mom relentlessly, begging her to please, please have a boy.

"Well, we'll just have to wait and see." She shakes her head. "It's not up to me."

So we wait and wait, until finally the day comes for her to go to the hospital. Kathy, Matt, and Lizzy leave for school, and my father, who has called in to work, is behind the bathroom curtain shaving when Gramma Murray arrives to take care of us as she has for every baby before. Mom is on the couch making strange breathing noises, and Gramma shouts to my father to hurry up and get his wife to the hospital before she has the baby right here.

After they leave, Gramma sends Michael out to her car to bring in her suitcase and the bags of supplies she brought along for her stay. Michael, with his slicked-back cowlick and new glasses, squares his shoulders for the task. He loves being the oldest one at home and moves from car to kitchen with a swagger of superiority. Gramma unpacks the bags—plastic containers filled with sugar cookies, peanut butter cookies with forked crisscrosses, and homemade fudge. We flock around her, smacking our lips as she hands out goodies to each of us.

I love Gramma. When she bends to hug me, she's all bosom and bad breath. She always has an apron tied around her boxy body, and she wears black tie shoes and thick stockings with dark lines that run up the backs of each leg and disappear under the hemline of her dress.

In the afternoon, my three older siblings bound off the bus and run up the driveway, shouting, "Did she have it yet? Did she have it yet? Is it a boy?"

When Gramma says, "no word yet," they exhale a collective sigh of impatience.

Finally, the phone rings just before supper, and we swarm to the kitchen, murmuring and pushing up against one another. Gramma puts her finger to her lips and lifts the receiver.

"Make it be a boy, make it be a boy," Kathy whispers as we wriggle together, bouncing on our toes, waiting for Gramma to hang up and give us the news.

"Well," she says with a smile. "Your baby brother's name is Simon."

We whoop and jump and join Kathy in a chant-like listing of our names, with the new one added at the end: *Kathy, Matt, Lizzy, Michael, Diane, Luke, Mary, Simon.*

Gramma laughs and shakes her head, arms folded across that large bosom.

"Okay, okay, get to the table now. It's time for supper," she shouts over the din.

I love Gramma's sugar cookies and homemade fudge, but her stew, I'm not so sure about. For one thing, the meat is stringy, and the beans and carrots are soggy. The peas bother me the most. Gramma uses the same canned peas Mom does— gray, slimy things with chalky skins that get caught in my teeth. My father has a Rule that we must eat everything on our plates. Gramma doesn't have that rule, but I don't want to hurt her feelings. I eat around the peas, and when she's not looking, I wad them up in my napkin and stuff them in the rat hole in the kitchen wall. I roll the baby's name over and over in my head. *Simon.* I decide I like it.

Gramma leaves when the baby—a fat little thing with tight fists and a full head of black hair—comes home. Mom moves Luke upstairs to free up a crib for the baby. He takes Kathy's spot in the bottom bunk next to me. On his first night, he and I giggle and hold hands across the divide until Kathy, now in the top bunk, leans over and says *go to sleep.*

I wake in the night to the muffled sounds of the new baby bleating in the bedroom below, and to Mary wailing that she misses Luke. My mother murmurs to both of them. In the morning, my father has already gone to work when I wake up. Mom is slumped half-asleep in a chair in the living room as Simon suckles from beneath a diaper she has draped over her shoulder to hide this business from us. She tells Kathy to get breakfast for us and snaps at me when I ask to look at the baby.

"Later." She pushes me away. "Now get to the table and eat your breakfast."

She points at Michael and says, "Go get your glasses." Michael hates his glasses, especially now that Kathy calls them Coke bottles and calls him Clarence the Cross-Eyed Lion. He stomps up the stairs, face bloated in a pout.

After the others catch the bus for school, Mom puts Mary in the playpen and tells Michael and me to keep an eye on her and Luke so she can get some work done. We pile on the couch to watch *Captain Kangaroo*, hooting as Ping-Pong balls rain down on Mr. Moose.

"See," I say to Michael later in the show. "Bunny Rabbit has glasses, too."

I mean it in a nice way, but my brother punches me in the arm, and Mom yells from the kitchen, "Hey, hey! No fighting." She is grouchy all day, and when the afternoon school bus pulls into the driveway, she is still dressed in her housecoat and slippers.

———————

My father disappears to the barns after supper, taking Kathy, Matt, and Lizzy with him. Every evening and all weekend they cut boards and hammer nails in preparation for the arrival of our milk cow. We have two barns, which we call the Front Barn and the Big Barn. The Front Barn sits at the top of the driveway—scruffy on the outside, cobwebby on the inside. The roofline extends to the right, sloping down to cover an open, dirt-floored area where an ancient tractor with flat tires sits. Wood-handled shovels and rakes hang from rusted nails along the back wall. Fixing the tractor is on a long list of projects my father talks about each night at the supper table.

A narrow door opens outward into the barn's main room, revealing a broken concrete floor and two cracked windows hidden behind stacks of dusty straw bales. My father sends my siblings to scout around the farm for odd bits of lumber and splintered boards, piecing them together to create an enclosure for several calves he says we are also getting. In the back corner of the barn, a steep open staircase leads upward to a low-raftered room filled with remnants of a chicken coop. Repairing the coop and getting chickens are also on the projects list.

Behind the Front Barn is a wide barnyard full of old farm equipment, and beyond that, the Big Barn. From a distance, the Big Barn looks massive and majestic in the way an elephant is massive and majestic. The wood siding is weathered to a soft gray and spotted with knotholes, and the tin gambrel roof twinkles in the sunlight. But a closer inspection reveals mismatched boards nailed all over the outside, covering up large holes in the walls. Inside, more disappointments: another cracked concrete floor in the milk parlor, more broken windows.

In the upper part of the barn, two giant wooden doors swing open to an uneven splintered wood floor. The twinkling roof leaks when it rains. That, too, goes on the projects list.

The much-anticipated day arrives. We are no longer just city people living in a farmhouse; today, we officially become farmers. My entire family waits at the edge of the driveway as the truck from the livestock auction house pulls in. Even Mom comes out of the house with Simon on her hip. My brothers chase behind the truck, turning nearly invisible in the dust rising from its tires. Kathy has Mary by the hand. Lizzy and I trot alongside the truck.

My father motions for the truck driver to stop near the Front Barn. We twirl and lick our lips, hovering while the driver unlatches the truck's tailgate and leads our new milk cow down the ramp on a braided rope. None of us have ever been this close to a cow, and we murmur and gasp at the black-and-white giantess with the prominent hip bones, spindly legs, and knobby knees. The animal is so tall I could walk underneath it if I had the nerve.

"Can we call her Bossie?" Lizzy is the first to bravely step up to the lumbering beast. She runs her fingertips up and down the furry slope of the creature's nose. Michael joins her, offering the cow a handful of pellets the man gives him. A tongue emerges from the animal's mouth, long and thick, dead-gray in color. I watch in fright, half expecting it to wrap around my brother's neck like the snake on TV did to the old man on *Wild Kingdom*.

"*Ewww*," Kathy says when the tongue touches Michael's hand. I'd bet he's scared, too, but Michael knows we are all watching, so he holds his hand there, letting the animal slobber it.

"It's wet and rough." He smirks at us, eyes magnified behind his glasses.

Mom takes Mary and Simon back to the house, and the rest of us form a procession behind my father and the man holding the rope as they lead our new cow to her new barn.

"Please, can we call her Bossie?" Lizzy asks again as we pass a shabby slatted corncrib on the edge of the barnyard and weave our way in and out of the farm equipment. The milk parlor is accessed through a heavy door that slides sideways on a track. My father pulls it open, and we follow him, the man, and the cow inside. The man guides the animal's head into one of the side-by-side wooden stanchions, clicking the lever in place so the cow cannot move its head. Lizzy hurries to put hay down, talking to the animal while she strokes its flanks.

"Do you like your new home, Bossie?" she asks. "Are you comfortable here?"

The cow lifts its tail in response, letting loose a load of stool that lands stinking and steaming in the gutter below.

Back at the truck, my father lets my older siblings bring the calves down the ramp. They take turns leading them—cute little things with curly hairs on their foreheads—into the Front Barn. I wait for my turn, but when the fifth and final calf comes to the back of the truck, my father grabs the rope, telling me I'm too small to do this. He and the calf disappear into the barn, joining my siblings, who are fawning over the animals.

Crushed and angry, I stay in the driveway by the truck ramp, sulking. I wonder how it is that I am big enough to look after Luke and Mary when the others are at school but not big enough to lead a calf by a rope.

At supper that night, my father announces a new Rule: If you're old enough to go to school, you're old enough to do chores. With that proclamation, he assigns duties. Kathy, now eight, is in charge of feeding the five calves and spreading fresh straw in their pens. Matt and Lizzy, seven and six, will milk Bossie. Before the sun rises the next morning, Mom comes up to the attic and shakes the three of them awake, whispering that it's time to get up for chores.

"Hurry now," she urges, "so you'll have time for breakfast before the bus comes."

They stumble sleepy-eyed in the dark, pulling on their clothes, and head down the stairs. I listen to their retreat from beneath my covers, imagining them in the utility room, putting on their work jackets and boots. I wait for the slam of the porch door.

An hour later, I am eating Sugar Pops at the table when they return from the barns. Mom shouts, "Don't spill it, don't spill it," as Matt walks carefully from utility room to living room to kitchen with the bucket of milk heavy in both hands. There are flies in the milk—some dead, others swimming for their lives—and cow hair, and speckles of dirt. Mom screens that all off, then pours the milk into the barrel of a little red-and-white machine and puts a lid on it.

"Don't worry," she says. "This pasteurizer will boil the milk and kill all the cooties."

The look on Kathy's face makes me wonder.

Later, after the school bus collects my siblings, and after the little machine hisses and steams, Mom lines up six green glass bottles on the counter, filling each with milk. She caps them and carries them in pot-holdered hands to the fridge, where they grow wide collars of cream that don't completely dissolve even when Mom shakes the bottles before pouring the milk into our glasses at lunch. She waves off my complaint that chunks of cream are floating in my glass and the milk tastes like the barn smells by saying, "Just drink it. It's good for what ails you." I don't say it out loud, but I miss the milkman, and his hat, and his milk.

Each morning and every night, my siblings return to the barns for chores. Despite my feelings about the taste and texture of this milk, I am struck by the ceremonial way Matt delivers it to my mother, and the responsibility he and Lizzy now carry instead of the milkman. The newness of these farming activities and the sense of importance for what they are doing create a ping of jealousy in me. I feel they are on a daily adventure I am not allowed to participate in because Mom decided it's too dangerous for me to go out to the barns. But it's that danger that makes me curious and makes the idea of being in the barns all the more enticing. Sure, I'm afraid of the dark, but I also ache for the thrill of going out into it.

The rhythm of our lives changes again when my father switches to the night shift at the factory. He calls it the graveyard shift and says this will free up his days to tackle the growing list of projects. It's strange to have him around all the time; before, he was mostly in the background of our lives, only home at night for supper and the *CBS Evening News* with Walter Cronkite. Now he seems to be everywhere. He arrives home around eight each morning, drops his lunch box on the kitchen counter, and sits at the table to wolf down a bowl of Bran Flakes, often in a bad mood, grumbling to my mother about how this job is killing him. His new work schedule spawns a new Rule: absolute quiet while he sleeps. He doesn't want to hear a *peep* from any of us once he disappears behind his bedroom curtain to lie down for a few hours. We try to be quiet, but even with three kids at school, there are still four of us and the baby in this small space, and Mom is constantly at us with her own scolding face, whispering, "*Shhh!* Quiet down or you'll wake your father."

When school lets out for summer, my siblings stay outside after chores, working alongside my father patching the barns and repairing the chicken coop. Michael turns five in July, making him old enough to go to school, and also (according to my father's Rule) old enough to do chores. He joins our older siblings outside, and I feel further abandoned, irritated by the distinction my mother is now making between the Big Kids and the Little Kids. She says I'll just get in the way if I go out to the barns, which only makes my curiosity grow about what is going on out there.

On the weekend, I watch from the open kitchen window as my father revs up the old tractor and backs it out from beneath the overhang of the Front Barn. A wide metal seat bounces up and down on a thick coil beneath him. The tractor's paint has faded so it is more pink than red, and the silver muffler on top is rusted through with holes, causing a deafening sound. The tractor spits, sputters, and stalls.

My father trims an old coffee can, wraps it around the muffler, and secures it with bits of wire, saying that'll keep the noise down. He pumps up the tires, jiggles some knobs, and restarts the engine. Black smoke billows from the muffler, but he's right—it is much quieter now.

He tells Matt to step up on the back of the tractor for a driving lesson, and they head into the side field, my father shouting instructions as my brother clings tightly to the seat of the tractor. They switch places for the return trip, and from the window, I marvel at my brother way up there on that wide seat. Matt's feet cannot reach the pedals, so he slides down to the edge of the seat to operate the clutch. The tractor lurches forward, careening across the open field as my seven-year-old brother bumps along, one arm wrapped around the bottom of the giant steering wheel, the other shifting gears. The sight both excites and frightens me.

Our windows rattle in resistance against the wail of the winter wind. Before the snow came, Mom had stapled heavy sheets of plastic around the insides of the window frames to keep the cold out. Now, the plastic slaps against the panes of glass where the air finds holes to blow through.

My teeth are clamped down on my tongue, the purple crayon in my fisted hand working to stay inside the lines. I lay splayed on the living room floor, just outside the kitchen doorway. My father and older siblings are outside doing the evening chores. Luke and Mary are in the playpen. The house is chilly and shadowy in the poor lighting, but it's peaceful. From my position here, I feel almost alone with my mother, who is at the stove stirring a pot of boiling potatoes with a wooden spoon as Simon rides on her left hip. I smile down at the finished page. All my colors are right: red flowers with green leaves, an orange sun, and white clouds in a sky I purposefully made purple. I excitedly take it into the kitchen to show my mother.

"Oh, that's nice, honey." She doesn't look at my coloring even though I am on my tippy-toes, holding the book up high for her. She bends to open the broiler door, pushing Simon back on her hip as flames shoot up around her hand when she brushes butter onto the chicken.

"Stand back," she warns me, pulling the broiler tray out to dab at the chicken in the very back. She closes the door, shifting my brother back to the middle of her hip, then stands to stir the potatoes again, as well as a smaller pot on a back burner that I hope isn't peas.

"What's taking them so long?" She frowns at the clock. "Supper's gonna be cold if they don't get in here soon."

She turns to me then, although I've already lowered and closed the coloring book.

"Put your coat on, Diane, and go tell Dad and the kids that supper is almost ready."

I hesitate at the surprise request.

"Go on," she coaxes, and as she smiles down at me, all the hurt I felt a minute ago about my coloring evaporates. Mom is asking *me* to go outside at night, asking *me* to go to the barns. I smile back at her, certain that she cannot know what a big deal this is for me.

"Try the Big Barn. Go on now, and button up your jacket. It's bitter cold tonight."

I leave the protection of the porch, pulling my hood up against the assault of the wind, and trudge across the driveway, listening to the *crunch, crunch* of snow beneath my boots. Overhead, the moon is full, like a perfect circle cut from black construction paper.

As I pass the Front Barn and make my way to the open expanse beyond, I turn to look behind me, feeling unsettled and less brave now that the house is no longer in view. In the barnyard, the ancient farm equipment lies asleep beneath a drift of snow. Hair rises at the nape of my neck as I hurry past all this stillness, certain a wild animal is crouched in the shadows, waiting to pounce and devour me. I try ignoring the thought of how my siblings would call me a scaredy-cat if they saw me here with my eyes darting around.

Grateful to see the light glowing from beneath the Big Barn door, I shake off my fear, thinking again how Mom has sent me out here at night by myself. Excitement returns with smug satisfaction. What are they all going to think when they see *me* here to tell them supper is ready? Me, the little sister who, until now, has been left out of all the Big Kid stuff.

I hear murmurs through the walls as I approach, and I picture them all in there, crowded around Bossie, taking turns sitting on the metal stool, spraying milk into the galvanized bucket below. Finally, I will be allowed a peek at the adventures they have been on out here; maybe I can even join in on the fun. Maybe my father will let me try to milk the cow. Maybe I'll get to help carry the pail of foamy milk into the house tonight.

I reach for the door handle but stop when I hear a muffled growl coming from inside. I pause, tilting my head to listen. The sound grows, but it isn't exactly a growl—it's more like the rumble of thunder. No. It sounds like shouting, and now I hear a scuffling noise, too. My heart hitches in my chest, my mind tumbling in confusion. I fight an urge to turn and run back to the house, to give up this Big Kid pretense and return to my coloring. I hesitate a moment longer as I summon bravery, then grip the handle with both hands, bend at the knees, and use all of my weight to slide the heavy door open.

Dusty yellow light from the barn pours out and over me. The first thing I notice as I blink and my eyes adjust is that there are mittens in the gutter—red mittens, blue mittens—mittens Gramma Murray knitted. I wonder who would put them there in that stinking mess. Something is not right here, and while I grapple with this image, I become aware of a vibration, like a soundless ticking, deep in my stomach. I suddenly feel groggy and disoriented, like the air has grown thick around me, as I stand frozen in the open doorway. Only my eyes move, lifting from the mittens and then traveling around the room, imprinting images onto my brain as though from a camera with a slow shutter speed.

Click: There is Lizzy cowering against the back wall, tears streaming down her face.

Click: And Michael, hunkered down in front of the stanchions, nearly out of sight.

Click: Matt on the floor at my father's feet. His arm bent to (shield?) his frightened face.

Click: My father, his back to me, casting a shadow over Kathy, who is also crying.

Click: Mittens in the gutter.

The growling—the rumble—is coming from my father. "Now, I've told you for the last time. I don't *ever* want to see *any* of you with mittens on in this barn. *Have you got that!?*"

Kathy trembles and nods in response. My father reaches out, shoving her so hard that she stumbles and falls onto the floor beside Matt.

"Answer me!" he bellows. "What's the Rule?"

"No mittens allowed in the barn." My sister's voice cracks and then breaks as she sobs.

My mind spins as I try to understand what is going on here. *Lizzy crying. Kathy crying. Michael hiding. Matt on the floor. Mittens in the gutter.*

My father whirls around to face me, purple-faced. Veins throb in his neck.

"Close that damn door. Can't you see you're letting the cold in?" His lips are pulled back tight against teeth, his eyes wild with fury. A monster's face.

In the horror of the moment, my brain is unable to translate what I am seeing. I can't move, rooted to my spot. Inside me, the ticking bangs against my ribcage.

"I said close the door. *Now!*" he roars, jarring me into action. I quickly pull the door closed, panic hammering at my chest and rising in my throat. The barn shrinks around me, trapping me here with this scary version of my father, this monster I have never seen before. In the silence, I watch him watching me.

Lizzy crying. Kathy crying. Matt on the floor.

"Mom said to tell you supper is ready," I blurt out, feeling the hollowness of the words hang in the noiseless air. I am not even sure if I am breathing.

Mittens in the gutter?

The eyes are still on me, eyes that I try to find my father in.

"Fine. Tell her we'll be there in ten minutes."

He scowls down at Matt. "Get up and finish your chores." He kicks my brother in the side of the leg. "And put your mittens in your pockets where they belong."

I leave the barn hurriedly and thankfully, rushing across the barnyard, tripping over deep ruts left by tractor tires on a warmer day, driven by a fear I have never known before. My mind wrestles with an onslaught of questions. *Was that really my father? With that loud, scary voice and that angry monster face? Did I really see him hit my siblings? A Rule about mittens? How could wearing mittens in the barn make him that mad?*

I think about how terrified my siblings looked. *Is this what happens in the barns all the time? The mystery I was dying to learn about?*

Back on the porch, I dawdle when taking off my jacket and boots, trying to catch my breath and understand what I just saw. Numb, except for the ticking inside of me that has not let up.

"Diane, is that you?" my mother calls out. "Did you tell them supper's ready?"

I walk slowly into the kitchen, wondering how to describe what just happened in the barn. I know my mother can explain this, make it right. I approach her, the words escaping me in a whisper: "Mittens in the gutter. Monster in the barn."

I look up at her. She purses her lips and studies me, her face now flushed. And then she turns from me.

"Quick, get the butter out for me. I have to get these potatoes mashed." She moves from stove to sink and back again, draining the water from the pot. "Please hurry," she urges, avoiding my stare and my fear. "I want to get supper on the table before I feed the baby."

I am already in my chair when my siblings swarm in, although I feel like a different person than I was before going out into the barn tonight. This new me is filled with heightened awareness—of every follicle of hair on my head, of where my skin ends, and the air begins—a keen awareness. This new me has new eyes that observe Matt and Michael fighting for the chair farthest away from the head of the table, where my father sits. And new ears that hear my mother tell Kathy to go and keep Simon quiet for a few minutes while she feeds the rest of us. The new eyes travel to the darkened doorway as my father enters; the new ears notice the immediate silence around the table. And lastly, these new eyes come to rest on my mother, who is getting my father his supper quicker than usual.

We bow our heads to recite the evening prayer: *Bless us, O Lord, and these Thy gifts, which we are about to receive from Thy bounty, through Christ our Lord. Amen.*

After we cross ourselves, I wait for someone to talk about it, about what I saw happen in the barn. We pass the chicken, potatoes, and corn around the table, and yet, no one speaks. Mom settles in her chair, adjacent to my father. I want her to question him about what I told her. I know I'll be less scared if she does. I want him to explain what he did and apologize to my siblings. And I want him to say it will never, ever happen again.

I push food around on my plate, searching my siblings' faces for an answer or even a clue. Each of them turns from my gaze, as though embarrassed. My father catches my eye.

"Finish your supper," he commands. His blue eyes are cold, narrowed at me as though in warning. Daring me, it seems, to say anything.

The panic I felt in the barn returns, *tick-ticking*, deep in my belly. And finally it hits me in a tidal wave of truth. It all makes sense. What happened in the barn is a *secret*, a secret I wasn't supposed to know about, not yet anyway. I understand that since I *do* know, I am expected to keep quiet, to pretend, just like the others.

As forks scrape plates and milk glasses are drained, the vibration inside of me becomes a painful hammering. We bow our heads and end the meal with another prayer.

Upstairs in the attic that night, the silence about what happened in the barn, the pretending, continues. I had hoped Kathy would talk about it, but neither she nor the others say a word about what I saw. I wonder if there is an unspoken rule about what can and cannot be talked about openly, what is allowed and what is forbidden to be shared.

I lay awake long after everyone falls asleep, trying to sort things out in my head. My mind keeps replaying scenes from the Big Barn, the things I witnessed for the first time in my life: fear on my siblings' faces, my father in a red-faced rage—a monster, violent and frightening. I start tying together the unsettling feelings I've had since our move to the farm and begin to recognize the impact moving has had, not just on me but on the rest of my family. The fact that my siblings don't come home to adoring neighbors who scoop them into their warm laps, and the realization that they no longer race around in the backyard with pals from the neighborhood. Here, there are no adoring neighbors or warm laps. There are no pals. Here, there is only us. Us, and this person my father becomes out in the barn, this monster that snuck in when I wasn't paying attention.

I make a deal with myself that from now on, I will be attentive to all actions, all words. I will learn to become vigilant, listen, and observe.

I hear the engine of my father's truck start up. He is off to work for the night.

Sleep finally arrives to suck me down, but before it does, I have one final thought: *Why didn't Mom say or do anything tonight?*

I wet my bed that night for the first time since getting out of diapers.

1964

Dressing Up in Church Faces

We take baths two at a time on Saturday nights because Mom says there isn't enough time or water for eight baths. Kathy is Mom's helper, toweling off Mary and Simon as Mom kneels at the tub. She adds Mr. Bubble and more hot water while Luke and I strip down for our turn. Once in, we make bubble beards and pass the bar of Ivory soap back and forth. We still don't have a door on the bathroom. Mom appears every now and then, pulling the curtain back to remind us to wash behind our ears and keep the water in the tub.

In the living room, the evening news ends, and *The Jackie Gleason Show* begins. I hear the band playing and know the June Taylor dancers are performing, gliding across the stage in their glittery sequins and feathered hats.

My father loves the show—he laughs when Ralph Kramden clenches his jaw and fists and tells his wife he's going to send her to the moon. I don't think it's so funny. I know he's only pretending, but the actor scares me with his loud voice and eyes that bug out of his head when he gets angry at Alice. I worry he really *will* hit her. *Pow! Right to the moon with you,*

Alice. My father wears that same face a lot, and when he does, there is no laughter from any of us.

Mom comes back in when the water gets cold. I hold a washcloth against my eyes to protect them from the sting of shampoo, *ouch-ouching* as her fingertips scrub my scalp. "Oh, stop it," she grumbles. "That doesn't hurt."

In the kitchen, she rolls my hair in small silver curlers. They pinch so tight against my scalp that when I lay my head on my pillow, it feels as though I have stones tied all around my head.

The entire family is up before the sun the next morning, getting ready for 6:30 mass. I ask Kathy to take my curlers out because she is gentler than Mom, unrolling them slowly so they don't tear my hair out. When she's done, I shake my head side to side, enjoying the tickle of the curls bouncing lightly against my face.

My brothers line up for Mom to slick their hair back with Brylcreem as my father paces in the living room, yelling that we are going to be late. Kathy hurries Mary and me into dresses while Lizzy rubs Vaseline on the toes of our black patent leather shoes to make them shine. It's still dark out when our Chevy leaves the driveway, my father at the wheel, his mouth a tight straight line across his face. There are ten of us in the car, but we are so quiet that I can hear the *crunch-crunch* of gravel as we pull out onto the road and head into town.

I watch my father's face change as he parades us down the church's center aisle to the very front rows (we take up two of them), nodding and grinning at the parishioners we pass, doing his peacock strut. The Big Kids sit in the front row, and Mom slides in behind them with Simon on her lap and Luke, Mary, and me squished between her and my father.

Michael fidgets during mass, making farting noises by rubbing his sweaty hand on the pew rail. He looks at Matt out of the corner of his glasses and they smirk, both trying not to laugh. Michael stops when my father pokes him in the back.

I can't blame my brother. Church gets pretty boring with Father Rowan up there on the pulpit droning on about how we are all sinners and how God will throw us into the fires of Hell if we don't obey Him. He has wet, saggy eyes and ends mass by saying, "Go forth and bear fruit." I watch my father sit up straighter, wondering why the two old ladies across the aisle are staring at my family and whispering.

Father Rowan stands on the steps outside, shaking hands with the parishioners as we file out. He says something about the blessings of all these gifts from God as he greets my parents. My father is once again a peacock and wears a grin I never see at home.

We pile into the car, Kathy in front between my parents with Mary on her lap. The rest of us nudge each other for room on the crowded back seat. My father wheels the Chevy out of the parking lot, and once we make the bend in the road and the church is out of sight, he slowly pulls over to the side. Off slips the Church Face and, swiftly twisting in his seat, he punches Michael right in the chest. My brother's glasses fly off his face and land in my lap.

"I *never* want to hear you making noise in church again. Have you got that?" My father is shouting out of his real face now as the cords on his neck strain against his tie. *Monster*, I think, terrified by this outburst. *Monster!*

Michael whimpers a yes, holding his hands to his chest.

"And *you* should know better than to encourage him." My father shakes his fist at Matt, then grabs the glasses from my lap and throws them at Michael.

"Now put these back on your face, and I don't want to hear a *peep* until we get home."

He spins back around and pulls onto the road. We ride home in silence. Not a word from my mother, frozen in her seat, eyes fixed on the windshield in front of her.

Later I search Kathy out. I want to ask her why my father's Home Face is so different from his Church Face. I want to ask her about what happened in the car, and why Mom never says or does anything. I want to know if she is as scared as I am. But when I finally get the chance to talk to her, the words cannot find their way out of my head and onto my tongue. The secret about what happens on our isolated farm has locked itself inside of me. Inside each of us. Not to be spoken, not to be discussed, even when it is right out in the open.

On cue from Father Rowan's *go forth and bear fruit* command, the sounds of retching begin again from the kitchen. I am not frightened this time. I don't sneak down the stairs to watch. I know what it looks like. But knowing doesn't stop me from wondering and worrying. Mom's last gift from God is only eight months old. And since his arrival, she has been in a bad mood a lot, sitting endlessly in the chair feeding him while shouting out orders to the rest of us: *Pick up your toys. Stop fighting. Go brush your teeth.* Maybe I'm jealous of Simon, the only one who gets any of her attention these days, tucked all snug under that diaper. Or maybe I just miss my old mother and my old house. Miss her singing while doing dishes, miss her sitting to relax and laugh over coffee with the Saunderses. Mom doesn't sing anymore. Or relax. Or laugh. And I'm thinking another baby is not going to help. It feels too soon for her to bear fruit again. This seems more like God punishing her than giving her a gift.

I lay in the shame of another wet bed, listening to the water rinsing the sink below, and then to the sound of Mom trudging up the stairs. I pretend to be asleep as she goes from bed to bed shaking my siblings awake.

"I'm already awake," Kathy snaps, and from the way she stomps around getting dressed, I know she heard the sounds coming from the kitchen too.

After they go, I strip out of my soggy pajamas, feeling especially bad for causing Mom more laundry today. The bare floor provides cold punishment to my feet.

Since the incidents in the barn and the car, I try to be invisible when my father is around. In the mornings, I play downstairs with Luke and Mary when the Big Kids leave for school. But when I hear his truck in the driveway, I clamber up the stairs to sit on the frayed rug between the bunk beds, trying not to make a peep. I hear the click of his spoon against his cereal bowl, he and my mother speaking in low voices. I put my ear to the floor the way Tonto puts his ear to the ground to listen for horses, straining to hear what they are saying. My mother is piling dishes in the sink, and over the din, I catch only a few of my father's words: *pigs, hay, another barn.*

I tiptoe down the staircase when I hear him snoring and come into the living room where Luke and Mary are together in the playpen. Mom is in her usual spot in the chair, a cloth diaper draped over Simon and her left breast. I ask if I can watch cartoons and she says, "Yes. Just keep it down so you don't wake your father up." Her voice sounds tired, even at this early hour.

We only get three channels, and I dial through the in-between ones, the ones that look like sheets of gray rain, until I get to *Captain Kangaroo* and raise the volume a teeny bit. Luke and Mary climb out of the playpen and join me on the floor. Mr. Green Jeans has three penguins with him today. Grandfather Clock's eyes move back and forth.

When my father wakes up, I escape again, this time to the outhouse. No one comes out here now that we have a real bathroom, so I have claimed this place as my own. Since the night in the barn, I come here to think about what is going on in my life and of all the changes that have happened since our move. I can't figure out if something was already in this new house—like an invisible poisonous gas that has infected my parents, causing my father to physically lash out and my mother to shut down—or if we unwittingly brought it along in our boxes. Whatever the cause, neither sunlight nor darkness changes it. I fret over the disruption in our lives and my parents' moodiness. Mostly, I worry about when my father is going to hit me.

I watch a fly circle and get caught in a spider web in the corner. The fly struggles, making a loud *bzzz bzzz bzzz*, like an SOS signal, as the spider races across the web, pounces on it, and then rolls it in silk, placing it at the edge of the web next to another cocooned victim. I feel like that fly. If I go *bzzz bzzz bzzz*, will anyone hear the alarm? Will anyone come to save me?

In the stillness of the outhouse, I feel the weight of my fears deep in my belly. A worry line creases my forehead as I draw my knees into my chest and wrap my arms around my legs.

The coop is ready, and the chickens arrive, dozens of them fluttering inside wire cages in the back of Willy Thompson's truck. Willy is a farmer from the next town over, jolly in a Santa kind of way, with the stub of a cigar always stuffed between the gap in his gray front teeth. His face is white-whiskered, his glasses held together at the bridge by black tape. He pulls his large body out from behind the steering wheel, steadying himself with a wooden cane. A hairy pink belly hangs visible beneath a tattered, ill-fitted T-shirt. We all like Willy despite his appearance, and we gather around him, his truck, and the commotion coming from the cages. My father shakes his hand, flashing the smiling face he wears to church.

"Gotcha fifty good egg layers." Willy's eyes twinkle behind greasy lenses. I love his big, hearty laugh and easy manner, so I move closer to him even though he stinks to high heaven.

Matt and Michael haul the cages out of the truck as white feathers fly everywhere. I reach out to catch one, tickling it against Mary's cheek to make her giggle.

Willy pulls the cigar from between his teeth and points it at a small wooden crate with two large, honking birds inside. He says, "Bring that one down, too." When Lizzy crouches to pet the soft plumage, a long neck with a bright orange beak draws back and strikes, snakelike, biting my startled sister. Lizzy yelps, scrambling away from the crate.

"Oh, ya gotta watch out for that gander, girlie," Willy warns. "He can be a sumbitch." He uses his cane to rap the bird on its beak before lifting the crate lid to free the pair. Fat, downy bodies on orange webbed feet jump out and take off running across the side yard, honking madly as they move in synchronicity toward the side field, tiny heads on long necks stretched skyward.

My brothers lug the chickens upstairs to the awaiting coop, and when Willy unwires the latches, they rush out, screeching and flying into each other. Feathers flutter and scatter before the birds finally settle down. They strut with their heads held high, red combs perched like hats on their heads. They seem to speak to one another in a slow drawl: *Bauuwck, bauwk, baaaauuwck.*

Back outside, my father pulls his wallet from his back pocket and counts bills into Willy's outstretched hand. Willy waves him off when he asks what he owes him for the geese.

"Nothin'." Willy laughs his wonderful laugh. "They're a gift from the missus and me. Raise yourself some little ones. They're good eatin'!" He plants the cigar back in its place between his teeth, climbs into his truck, and backs down the driveway. My siblings all wave and shout goodbye to Willy, but my eyes are on my father. As the farmer's truck disappears up the road, so does the smile on my father's face.

"Come on," he says to the Big Kids. "Time to get back to work."

I slink off, relieved once again to still be one of the Little Kids.

Untangling the old farm equipment in the barnyard is on the list of summer projects. My father plans to cut the overgrown alfalfa in the fields to feed the cows. He and the Big Kids work on the rusted machinery one piece at a time. Some of the equipment comes back to life; the rest should have been left to sleep where it lay. They hook the hay mower with its new blades to the back of the tractor and Matt heads out to begin mowing the side field. From the swing set in the backyard, I watch him driving back and forth, back and forth. The mower extends behind him as alfalfa falls neatly to the ground with each pass; the air smells sweeter than freshly-cut grass.

When the mowing is finished, Matt takes the hay rake out to the field. The rake looks like a rusted rack of ribs between two large metal wheels. The clumsy contraption rattles along behind the tractor, scooping up hay and setting it back down into tidy rows. When my father is inside sleeping, Michael runs behind the rake chasing the mice and field voles that scurry out from beneath the lifted hay. He stomps on them, dangling the critters by their tails and shouting, "I got another one!"

The hay baler is dislodged from its spot in the barnyard, a complicated piece of machinery that looks to me like a small, lusterless, wingless airplane. It needs a lot of repairs, and my father chooses Kathy as his helper to fix it, sending my sister to the porch to dig through random tools looking for a wrench, a screwdriver, or whatever other tool he needs. The baler is still broken on the second day of repair, and my father grows more frustrated, cursing and yelling at my sister if she brings the wrong wrench. He kicks her, screaming that she better move a little faster. Kathy cries out with each blow. I see and hear it all from way back in the yard where I sit stiffly on a swing, my stomach churning with fear. I scuff the dirt at my feet, not wanting to move, afraid the swing will squeak and draw attention to me.

My father is still yelling as he climbs in his truck, slams the door, and tears down the driveway. Off to Agway to buy another replacement part. Once his truck is out of sight, Lizzy and Michael poke their heads out of the barn where they have been shoveling cow manure.

"Come on out," Kathy coaxes. "It's safe."

They run to the backyard to join me on the swing set. Kathy is limping, but she also has a smirk on her face. They are not supposed to play when he's gone—it's a Rule—but my siblings do it every chance they get. I offer my swing to Kathy, feeling as though I am in cahoots with her and the others. She looks at her wristwatch, calculating the amount of time they have before he returns. From our position in the yard, we can see a vehicle coming long before it can see us, so when the blue Ford comes into sight a while later, they scatter back to their work. When my father pulls into the driveway, he is none the wiser. I like this secret and find their act of defiance deeply satisfying.

It is early evening when the baler is finally working. After chores and supper, my father and the Big Kids attach it to the tractor and then hook a rickety hay wagon behind it. The wagon is long and broad, with a wood-planked floor, a tall wood-slatted backboard, and four metal wheels. The tractor, the baler, and the wagon move together like a train, bumping out into the field. My father is in front on the tractor, my four siblings clinging to the wagon's backboard.

Once in the field, Matt drives the tractor, and my father gets on the wagon with the others to show them how to stack the bales of hay properly. My six-, seven-, and nine-year-old siblings struggle under the weight of the bales as my father cuffs them, shouting "move faster" and "straighten that bale."

Heavy summer rains keep my father irritated. At supper, he speaks directly to Matt about how the wet fields have slowed the harvest. I listen to the exchange, noticing how grown-up my eight-year-old brother looks. Matt, deeply sunburned, speaks in a serious tone, assuring my father that the hay will be in before the end of summer.

Three days of sunshine keep my father and the Big Kids in the fields until dusk. I try to block out the sounds of my father screaming at them, sounds that carry through the screened windows of the house. Even though I am safe here inside, my heart thumps against my ribs.

After they leave the field, and after they unload the final wagon, sending the bales up the grain elevator to the mow in the Big Barn, they go about their evening chores, which now take even longer. Besides the chickens, which are Kathy's responsibility, my father also bought four pigs recently, giving their care to Michael. It is well after dark before they finally come in for supper, haggard with their hair full of dust and hay, their arms scratched and bleeding. Thick, yellow calluses have formed on the pads of their palms from the hay bale ropes.

My father carries his foul mood across the threshold, cursing the weather report of overnight rain. He knocks Michael clear off his chair when my brother accidentally spills a glass of milk. *But the milk is free!* I want to shout. *Why did you do that when the milk is free?* I wonder about my mother, passing around the breaded pork chops, the mashed potatoes and butter, the green beans. Saying nothing about what is happening in our kitchen.

We bow our heads. We recite the Lord's Prayer. We say "Amen."

———

It rains all night. In the morning, the sun hides behind dark clouds. After chores, the Big Kids join the rest of us at the table for breakfast. We pass around Sugar Pops and Corn Flakes and scoop heaps of sugar on top. No fights this morning. We are all watching the clock, waiting for the truck to come up the driveway, readying ourselves for my father's mood.

Mom finishes breastfeeding Simon, puts him back in his crib, then filters the flies, cow hair, and dirt from the milk pail, moving quickly through her own routine. She has a doctor's appointment this morning, which explains the pin curls usually reserved for church days. After switching the pasteurizer on, she puts Mary in the high chair and tells Kathy to feed her, then disappears behind her bedroom curtain to get dressed.

We listen together to the sound of the truck, and the porch door slamming, and then the *thump, thump* of my father's boots as he kicks them off onto the utility room floor. I feel the air thicken and the low *tick, ticking* inside of me. From the bedroom, the ping of bobby pins rings out as they drop into the tin Mom stores them in.

When my father takes his seat at the head of the table, Lizzy jumps to get the Bran Flakes and his special cereal bowl.

"Here you go, Daddy." She smiles, placing a big spoon and a bottle of milk next to his bowl. I've noticed this about my sister lately, how she steps in to try to placate my father with kind words and gestures.

Mom comes out of the bedroom, clipping earrings to the lobes of her ears. I have never seen my parents hug or kiss one another. Kathy says my mother used to call my father Ricky, but that was back in our old house, and I don't remember it. Here, they rarely exchange morning greetings when he comes home from work.

"You remember I have a doctor's appointment, right?" Mom says as my father's spoon clicks against his bowl. "I'm leaving Kathy in charge of the Little Kids."

My father lifts the bowl to his lips and drains the milk before responding. We are all dillydallying with our own cereal bowls, waiting for him to excuse us from the table. I am already fretting about what the day holds for us, alone here with him.

"The fields are too wet for haying." He wipes the back of his hand across his mouth. "Take them all with you so I can get a few decent hours of peace and quiet."

Mom runs a wet washcloth over Mary's face. "Richard, I can't take all these kids into the doctor's office with me." She lifts my sister from the high chair and carries her to the playpen in the living room.

"Get your shoes on. All of you," my father says. "You're going with your mother."

I try concealing my excitement as I carry my bowl and spoon to the sink, feeling light inside at the possibility of going somewhere other than church, *and* without my father. I slip my shoes on, waiting with Luke for Kathy to tie them. Mom is still resisting, telling him the doctor was not happy the last time she brought us kids to the visit with her.

"You'll all behave for your mother, right?" My father stands in the utility room doorway, hands on hips. When we give our absolute assurance, he turns to my mother and says, "See?"

Mom sighs, muttering under her breath as she returns to her bedroom to get Simon up. Despite her reaction, we pile into the Chevy, giddy for the adventure. Kathy sits up front holding the baby, with Luke and Mary squashed together between her and Mom.

Lizzy lets me have the window, and I kneel on the back seat, watching as the open fields give way to large houses with long, paved driveways sporadically dotting the landscape. We come over a rise, and there is the city with its tall brick factories and numerous bridges zigzagging across the Genesee River. The road narrows here with two-story houses crowded shoulder to shoulder. The sky has cleared and ladies in light sweaters sit in clusters on the wide-railed porches.

I like the bustle of the city, the traffic lights swinging at the intersections, the cars bumper-to-bumper on the road. Businessmen hurry along the sidewalks and groups of kids scoot around them, laughing and chasing each other. Lizzy rolls the window down when we pass Highland Park so I can stick my nose out and smell the lilacs that grow in abundance there.

My mother steers the car into a parking lot and shuts off the engine. She bends the mirror toward herself and applies dark-red lipstick, first to the top lip and then to the bottom. I love watching her draw it on, and the small sound of the smack of her lips. She is dressed in her Sunday clothes, her shoulder-length auburn hair thick and curly. I think she looks beautiful.

Mom says we are going to stay in the car while she's inside. She pulls a roll of Necco Wafers from her pocket, holding up the bribe as we *ooh* and *aah*.

"You can have these if you're good for Kathy." All eyes are on the roll as she passes it to my sister, who assures Mom we will be fine. Mom turns in her seat. She doesn't seem convinced. "Please behave for your sister. I won't be long."

We promise we will be good, but we grow restless quickly, all eight of us trapped in the car. Kathy raises the roll of Necco Wafers, reminding us that if we behave, we can have one. We all shout that we want the chocolate one, except Lizzy, who likes the black one that tastes like licorice. Kathy says, "No, you'll eat the one you get." I squint hard at the waxed paper, trying to count down to the one that will be mine, hoping it is the chocolate wafer.

We sing "Row, Row, Row Your Boat" in rounds, and when we get bored with that, Kathy leads us in "Bill Grogan's Goat." It is a funny song about a goat that eats red shirts. We repeat each verse after my sister, giggling when Luke and Mary mess up the words. But even that gets boring after a while and we fall off one by one.

Michael complains that Matt won't let him have the window seat, and they start to push and punch each other, ignoring Lizzy's pleas for them to stop. Kathy lets Michael climb over to the front, and he slides into the driver's seat, grabs the huge steering wheel, and pretends he's driving. He presses on the horn twice and a lady in the car parked next to us frowns.

Kathy makes Michael return to the back seat, and he is pouting there when Luke points out the window and shouts, "A balloon! A balloon!"

We all look, and sure enough, a giant oblong gray balloon is way off in the sky, floating toward us. Its enormity takes my breath away.

"That's not a balloon." Kathy laughs. "It's called a blimp."

The thing moves at an agonizingly slow speed. When it finally gets close enough, Lizzy reads the words on the side of it out loud: *Good Year.*

We squeal and jump around, begging Kathy to let us out so we can see it better. It takes a lot of convincing, but she finally gives in, warning us that if we don't behave, we will have to get back in the car. We open the doors and bound out. Kathy places Mary on the hood of the car, and Luke and I scramble up next to her. The three of us lay down with our backs against the windshield, me in the middle to hold their hands. Lizzy is in front of us and Michael and Matt perch with their legs dangling over the headlights. We watch in awe, faces upturned, as the massive thing approaches.

Kathy stands next to the car, rocking Simon in her arms. She tells us that blimps are filled with a gas called helium and that's what makes them float. She says people get to ride in the little box hanging from the bottom. Kathy seems to know about everything, and I can't wait to start school soon so I can be as smart as she is.

The mammoth vessel travels right over our heads, cloaking us in its shadow. It sounds like it is breathing. I wave my hand, hoping one of the people will see me and wave back. It is a moment of joy like I have never experienced. Lizzy draws her knees up to her chest and wraps her arms around them. Her mouth is agape. Beneath her dark bangs, her eyes follow the blimp as it moves slowly, slowly across the sky. "I want to ride in a blimp." She sighs.

————————

Summer is nearly over, and the pressure is on to get the rest of the hay in before school starts. At breakfast, my father says it's *all hands on deck now*. He points his cereal spoon at me.

"You're going to school this year, right?" He doesn't wait for me to respond. "Yes, you are, so I want you out on the hay wagon now."

"Now?" I ask, startled by this sudden decision. I'm still four and terrified of being around him outside with the Big Kids. *What if I do something to make him mad? Will he hit me? Will he kick me with his steel-toed boot? What will that feel like?*

I look to my mother, hoping she will step in and say I'm too little, but she is distracted this morning. Luke is in bed with a high fever and Simon is teetering about, practicing his new walking skills. The new baby is due any day and Mom has been especially cranky, waddling around the house with her giant belly, impatient with us and our constant nagging for reassurance that this one will be a girl to continue our girl-boy pattern.

"Yeah, now." My father turns to Matt. "She can help you unload the wagons." And just like that, I am enlisted to work outside.

The day is blistering hot, the air sticky and still. Despite the heat, I am dressed in heavy dungarees, only vaguely aware of the sweat trickling down the backs of my legs and pooling in my white ankle socks. I can't lift the hay bales because they weigh more than I do, so Matt shows me how to drive a hay hook into them to drag them. It takes all my strength, and I need both hands on the hook's wooden handle to accomplish this, so I am slow in getting them to the front of the wagon. There, Matt lifts them onto the elevator to ride along rusted chain tracks, upward to the haymow's open window.

The elevator—a long, narrow, battered contraption on two wheels—was resurrected from the barnyard with the other old equipment. It is actually too short to reach the window; it only does so because my father put it on concrete blocks to give it more height and then raised the nose to its steepest angle.

The noise from the elevator makes it impossible to talk to one another without shouting. It creaks and moans under the weight of the hay, and the steep angle puts added strain on the motor. Because of the steepness, bales slide back down every now and then, toppling over the side, breaking the ropes, and spilling hay all over the ground. When this happens, my father crouches in the small window above, sweat pouring off his long, hooked nose, and screams, "Goddammit, Matt, be careful! Load them straight!"

I feel bad for my big brother, who is doing most of the work. He loads three bales onto the elevator for each one I bring him, keeping calm even when my father yells. Once the wagon is unloaded and the elevator is turned off, he smiles and tells me I did a great job. Another wagon appears with Kathy at the wheel of the tractor, and Lizzy and Michael sitting on top of the load, six tiers off the ground. They hold on tightly as the wheels move over the barnyard's uneven ground, which tips the wagon precariously to one side.

The day unfolds in a frenzied game of beat the clock as they harvest, and we unload wagon after wagon. In the afternoon, my father's voice booms over the racket of the elevator. "Matt, I need you up here with me. Diane, go tell your mother to come out and help."

I scamper to the side of the wagon, dust scattering around my red Keds as I drop to the ground and take off running for the house. Inside, Mom stirs Campbell's chicken noodle soup on the stove, her remedy for Luke's fever, her pregnant belly dangerously close to the flame. She stops as she hears the request, wooden spoon in the air, her lips pressed together.

She appears frozen in a pause—a rare change from her usual perpetual motion, face gone slack, eyes blank. She blinks twice and starts to move again.

"Mary, put your sneakers on," she calls to my two-year-old sister, who is in the playpen with Simon. To me, she says, "Come help me."

She lifts Simon out of the playpen and then she and I tip the heavy wooden thing upside down and over him, creating a cage to keep him corralled. He whimpers in protest, even when I crouch down and push toys through the bars to him as I've seen Mom do.

"I'll be back soon," my mother coos, handing him a bottle of warmed milk. "Be a good boy."

She tells me to take Mary with me and says she'll be right out after she gives Luke the soup. I leave her in the utility room, leaning over that big belly to pull on her loafers, and race back to the barnyard hand in hand with my sister. Matt reaches down to hoist us up on the wagon, and I resume dragging bales to the front, now with Mary's help.

My father leans out of the haymow window and shouts down. "Where is your mother? Did you tell her to come out here?"

I nod, cupping my hands to my mouth, and shout back, "Yes, she's on her way."

When Mom arrives, she has trouble getting up onto the wagon because of her belly. Matt lowers a bale of hay to the ground to give her more height, and she uses it as a step, steadying herself with her hands on the floor of the wagon so she can pull her body up. Seeing my mother like this, on her hands and knees, makes my eyes water. I'm grateful when Matt helps her to her feet. I can't hear what he says over the screeching elevator, but she waves him off and lumbers over to the pile of hay. Matt hops off the wagon and runs to the barn.

Mom has difficulty keeping her balance, and when she leans forward to place a bale of hay into the elevator's tracks,

I worry she will tumble off the wagon. The first two bales go up fine, but the third one slips from her grip, landing sideways on the elevator. She is unable to right it, and halfway up, the bale turns completely and falls to the ground, ropes breaking, hay scattering.

"Keep them straight, Rose," my father yells from above.

I move in to help her situate the next bale more solidly on the elevator, afraid I might fall myself. Mary and I bring the bales right to my mother's feet so she doesn't have to move around too much, and the three of us progress as well as we can, but we are much slower than Matt was. My father keeps yelling "Faster! Faster!" and "Get a move on down there!"

We try to move faster, but we are exhausted. Mom holds the bottom of her belly with one hand while she and I wrestle another bale onto the elevator together. As the bales go up, crooked ones fall off, exploding to the ground.

My father's rage continues. "Goddammit, Rose. Keep them straight!" His face is darker each time it appears at the window. From the sky, the sun punishes us further.

I am the first to see the man standing in the barnyard with his hands on his hips. Because of the noise from the elevator, it is difficult to know how long he has been there or what he has heard. It is Bob O'Donnell, a neighboring farmer. He gives nothing away from behind his dark sunglasses. My stomach flips over and I quickly look up at the window, relieved that it is empty.

Mr. O'Donnell moves toward us, a handsome tight-muscled man with a headful of wavy brown hair and an uncanny resemblance to our recently deceased president, John Kennedy. My sisters and I all have crushes on him. He is almost to the wagon before Mom looks up, and when she sees him, she blushes right down to her collar.

"What are you doing out here in your condition?" he shouts up to her. Mom's eyes grow wide, and she quickly looks up toward the window.

"We need to get the hay in," she shouts back. Then, she bends with me to push another bale onto the elevator. It begins to turn sideways, and Mr. O'Donnell jiggles it back into place, his face still turned toward my mother. I move to the back of the wagon to help Mary drag another bale up front, and although I can't see his eyes, I know he is watching us, too.

"Where are the other little ones?" he shouts.

"In the house," she responds, blushing deeper.

"Alone?" his eyebrows rise behind the glasses.

She nods, and he shakes his head, frowning.

"Go back inside. I'll finish up here," he shouts and reaches for her hand to help her down.

I look back up to see my father now framed in the window with his own frown.

"No, I'm fine." Mom bends to lift the next bale but Mr. O'Donnell leaps on the wagon, takes it from her, and tosses it onto the elevator. He sees my father, gives him a quick wave, and turns back to my mother.

"Go on, Rose. I'll finish up here with the girls."

She argues further but he steers her to the edge of the wagon and gently helps her down.

Red-faced, my mother thanks him and then hurries across the barnyard, head bent low, never looking back. My father's eyes narrow and follow her.

"Hey Bob!" he shouts down. "What are you doing sending my help away?" He has his Church Face on now. Mr. O'Donnell does not smile back.

"I'll finish the work for her," he shouts, plucking a bale of hay off the floor of the wagon, deftly tossing it onto the elevator.

"Okay. Just try to keep up the pace," my father shouts back. "It's hotter than hell up here." He disappears from the window.

Mr. O'Donnell strides to the back of the wagon where Mary and I are struggling to drag another bale forward.

"Why don't you girls take a break?" He leans in so we can hear him. "Go ahead. Sit down on that bale of hay for a few minutes." He smiles and points to a lone bale up front. We've been taught to obey adults so we sit side by side on the bale, even though I worry we will get in trouble for it later. Mr. O'Donnell moves to the back of the wagon, muscles bulging as he lifts bale after bale, tossing them expertly onto the elevator. I have never seen a wagon empty so quickly, and I fall a little more in love with him. We stand up so he can load this final bale, and when that one disappears through the window, he descends from the wagon and turns the elevator off.

In the sudden silence, we hear my father's muffled voice yelling at Matt to keep stacking. Mary and I scramble off the wagon as Mr. O'Donnell wipes his brow. He bends down and says, "You girls did a great job."

I blush, feeling all soft inside. We say "thank you" in unison.

My father appears, his shirt sticking to him. Sweaty dust glistens in the hair on his arms.

"Well, Bob, you sure move faster than Rose." His Church Face laughs.

Mr. O'Donnell pulls a cigarette from his shirt pocket. He doesn't laugh back or shake my father's extended hand. He strikes a match, lights the cigarette, and inhales deeply.

"You really kept us hopping up there." My father pulls a handkerchief from his back pocket and wipes it across his face.

Mr. O'Donnell lets a long stream of smoke out of the side of his mouth. My father hates cigarette smoke and the Church Face falters as the smoke dissipates slowly in the still air.

"Just trying to help you out, Richard," the farmer says quietly.

My father puts his hands on his hips, squaring his shoulders up under his thick neck.

"Yeah, and I appreciate that, Bob. But I don't want my kids thinking they can sit around while somebody else does the work." He hooks his thumb in our direction but does not mention my mother.

Mr. O'Donnell remains silent behind the sunglasses, the cigarette burning in his right hand.

My father turns to us. "Go tell your mother to send some Kool-Aid out."

We gratefully scamper off, leaving the two men staring at one another.

On the morning of my first day of kindergarten, Mom shakes me awake with the Big Kids for chores. Gone are the naive notions I once held about them being on adventures. I rise with a sense of doom, knowing I am one of them now.

My father has decided that I will take over feeding the pigs so Michael can care for the calves in the Front Barn. I follow my brother to the corncrib with a dented metal bucket. He tells me the pigs get four of these with each feeding. I have trouble lifting the pail and worry out loud that it's too heavy for me. Michael turned six in July. He is tough and mean.

"Too bad," he shrugs, "You might have to make more trips with less corn in the bucket."

He takes it from me, lugs it to the pen, and empties it into the trough. Squealing, the pigs rush around him, pinning him between them as they gobble it up. Michael pushes back against them with his hips. The pigs live in a tiny tar paper-roofed building behind the Front Barn with a doorway so low we have to duck to get inside. Outside, a three-railed wood fence surrounds their pen.

Michael shows me how to draw water from the old hand pump at the back of the barnyard. I watch his arms shake under the weight as he lifts the pail with both hands, up and over the fence. It takes several trips to fill the water trough, and once again, the pigs crowd around him, their fat, bristled bodies pushing up against him and each other. I don't like their greedy, beady little eyes. Their wet snouts. When they won't move, Michael pounds them on the back, muttering, "Goddamn pigs." Michael has started swearing recently, only in front of us, of course, but I am still impressed. It makes me feel like he's getting away with something the rest of us are too afraid to try.

After chores, I follow the others into the house to wash up, eat breakfast, and wait at the end of the driveway for the bus. I grip Kathy's hand, nervous and excited when the yellow door swings open. I climb the tall steps one at a time and continue holding my sister's hand when we stand in line outside St. Bernadette School, waiting for the bell to ring.

"That's your teacher, Mrs. Walters." Kathy points to a lady with gray hair and steel-rimmed glasses. My teacher shakes hands with parents, then ushers them and their kids into her room.

"This is my sister, Diane," Kathy says, handing me off to this smiling woman in the navy skirt, white ruffled blouse, and thick, black shoes like Gramma's.

"Welcome to kindergarten." Mrs. Walters gives me a warm smile, easing my fears. I shuffle into the room, already crowded with other kids and parents taking photographs, combing hair, and smoothing dresses. Three of the girls cling to their mothers, crying. I watch these mothers wipe tears from their daughters' faces, hugging them and promising them they are going to have a fun day. Something stirs inside of me as I observe these well-manicured mothers and the dads in crisp shirts and neckties, all kneeling before their children, kissing them on their foreheads. It is a new sensation, hot and dark. I stand in the crowd feeling out of place.

Unsure of what to do, I wind through the congestion to the back of the room where the sun pours through floor-to-ceiling windows encased in thick oak wood. Shelves along the wall hold neatly arranged toys and round bins of crayons. A narrow bookcase runs the length of the front wall. I trail my finger along the spines of the books—I have never seen so many.

Five low circular tables fill the center of the room. I spy the one with my name written on a tented piece of cardboard and sit on a red chair, swinging my legs, trying to look as though I feel comfortable. Other kids find their places around the tables, and when a girl sits at the tent that says "Leslie," we smile at each other.

Once Mrs. Walters gets the lingering parents to leave, she gathers us around her on the floor for Circle Time. She asks us a bunch of questions about what we can and can't do. I am embarrassed to find I am the only one who cannot tie her own shoes. Mrs. Walters points at pictures in a book, asks us what the objects are and what colors they are. Excited hands shoot up as kids shout out the answers. I am too shy to do that even though I know it's a gray elephant.

Kindergarten is only a half-day, and I ride the bus home with Leslie, my first friend. I can't wait to tell Mom about her and about my amazing day. I take the steps off the bus one at a time, holding tightly to the silver handrail, and say goodbye to Mr. Glenn, the bus driver. I bound across the yard and onto the back porch, shouting "I'm home!" as I come through the door and into the utility room. I kick my shoes off there, and when I see my mother hurrying from the kitchen toward me, I break out into a giant grin. But then something strange happens—everything slows way down. Mom rushes across the living room, but she is moving in slow motion with her arms extended in front of her big belly. And maybe it is because of all that I have seen and felt today—parents kissing and hugging their kids, the excitement of the first day of school—that I believe she is reaching for me, bending to scoop me into her arms. This is what I think as I rush, also in slow motion, toward her outstretched arms, filled with a dizzying bliss. But now her right arm rises up, bending at the elbow. She draws her index finger toward her mouth, her eyes wide. Her other hand reaches up, also in slow motion. I think it is going to pull me into an embrace, but it grabs me gently by the shoulder, stopping me.

"*Shhh*," she whispers, her index finger pressed to her lips. "I just put the other kids down for their naps."

We had counted on the new baby being a girl. We even named her Janet. So when Gramma hangs up the phone and announces it's a boy, we sit in stunned silence.

"It can't be a boy," Kathy complains. "We've been girl, boy, girl, boy all the way so far. A boy will ruin our record."

"Well, I'm sorry you wanted a girl." Gramma shrugs and moves around the table ladling out beef stew. "But your mother just said to tell you that you have a baby brother, and his name is Joseph, not Janet. You'll call him Joey."

The news is devastating—at least, that is what Kathy tells us upstairs as she helps Mary into her pajamas while the rest of us prepare for bed. Mary is up here now to make room for the new baby. She, Luke, and I sleep in the bottom bunks, Matt, Lizzy, and Michael above. Kathy has moved to an old olive-colored army cot under the front window.

"He's ruined *everything*," she tells us as she perches on the edge of Mary's bed, arms folded across her chest. We huddle on the lower beds, listening to our big sister complain. As our lives have become more strained, we've begun deferring to Kathy for what to say, how to behave, how to feel about things. If she is upset, we get upset. If she thinks something is funny, we laugh. She is our collective emotional barometer, and we trust her completely. So when Kathy tells us we need to call this baby Janet when it comes home, we agree.

My father doesn't come home on two of the three nights my mother is in the hospital. He is working the day shift again at the factory. Chores are easier without him here constantly yelling at us, and our house feels more relaxed. But it's strange not having him at home in the evening. On the first night, Gramma keeps his supper warming on the stove until it gets really late, and then she tells us he probably stayed overnight in the hospital with my mother. When he doesn't come home the second night, she says maybe he's visiting at the hospital and will be home later. But I don't hear his truck come home, or leave the next morning, and when I go downstairs, I peek through the curtain into his bedroom to find the bed still made.

"He called to tell me he was out all night playing poker with his buddies," Gramma answers when I ask.

"I didn't know he played poker," Lizzy pipes in. "Who does he play with?"

"You ask too many questions. Mind your own business now and eat your breakfast," Gramma says. "Your mother will be home soon with the baby."

She brings a plateful of toast with melted butter and cinnamon sugar to the table. We grab at pieces, shoving them whole into our mouths. I savor the sweetness of the concoction, stuck for just a moment to the roof of my mouth.

"And you'd all better be nice to that baby," Gramma warns, but with a smile.

1965

Go Get the Club

M y first attack comes neither from hand nor boot. Lizzy and I are helping our father build an expanded enclosure for the pigs behind their barn. We tore the old wooden fence down and Michael is busy carrying the debris off to a burn pile in the side field. My job is bringing two-by-fours to the sawhorses where my father cuts them into pointed three-foot stakes. This is my first time working on a project with him, and I am fretting about getting hit. *When will it happen?* I worry as I carefully hand the boards to him. *Will I see it coming? Will there be any warning, or will he just draw his leg back and kick me across the barnyard?*

When all are cut, Lizzy holds the stakes in place as my father pounds them into the ground around the barn. We unspool the roll of heavy-gauge wire my father got from Agway, and he attaches first one strand and then another to each stake until the entire area is fenced in. I don't understand how wire is going to keep the pigs in better than the wooden fence, but I don't dare ask and risk upsetting my father, who, so far, has not yelled at or touched any of us.

After the stakes are strung, he affixes a small, black metal box to the wall in the Big Barn, running more wire from the box to the pig fence. He calls the box an electric charger. I still don't get it, but I watch the box with interest as a red light blinks on and off and the green light beneath it comes to life.

"Now let's go see if it's working." He leads us out of the barn and back to the barnyard.

"Diane, come over here." He moves closer to the fence, motioning for me to join him.

I take tentative steps, wary of his smile that's not really a smile.

"Come on," he coaxes. "I'm not gonna bite you."

He turns to Lizzy and Michael and says that since I am the one in charge of the pigs, it only seems right that I should be the first to *test* the new fence.

"Don't you agree?" he asks them.

Michael nods, his eyes wide behind his glasses, but Lizzy is chewing her lower lip, which worries me further. My father looks down at me with that smile and says, "Go ahead. Wrap your hand around the wire." I wrinkle my brow, feeling that familiar vibration start up inside my ribcage. The wire looks harmless, but this still feels like a trick.

"Go on," he says. "Just grab ahold of it."

I reach for the top strand of wire, taking it into my right fist. The shock is strong and immediate—like a million pin pricks on my palm. It pulses up my arm and spreads through my body, causing my muscles to jump in sharp, painful bursts. I yelp and tumble to the ground, holding my tingling hand as my father's shadow falls on me, the smile on his face now wicked.

"I guess it's working," he says calmly. "That should keep the pigs in, huh?"

I am unable to answer him because I am dizzy, not just from the physical shock of what happened but from something deeper inside of me. I had been anticipating this day, waiting for the slap on the back of the head, the punch in the shoulder, or worse, the kick with that steel-toed boot. I had fretted mostly about what that boot might feel like—the force of it powerful enough to lift me off the ground as I'd seen it do to my older siblings, and me going *oof* like they do. I had worried about what mistake I would make to anger him enough to finally lash out at me, but I hadn't seen this one coming. I hadn't done *anything* to anger him, hadn't seen *any* warning of what was to come. I sit in the dirt, wordless and stunned, as he turns and walks away.

"Are you okay?" Lizzy reaches to help me off the ground, her face pale with concern.

I say I am even though I feel the tickle of imminent tears at the corners of my eyes. But then something strange happens, also unforeseen and unfamiliar. The drumming inside of me stops abruptly, and I feel a new sensation rising, like a black funnel cloud swirling inside. Anger of a kind I have never felt before, a deep-in-the-bones anger. My face is hot with it, brows knitted together with it. I dust off my dungarees, my lips now pressed tightly together. The thought of crying is long gone, way in the distance behind me, and now I am worried I might scream and release this black funnel cloud in a torrent of ugly, dangerous words, launching them like stones across the barnyard. Pelting *him*, hurting *him*. I struggle to control this rage, this snapping dog at the end of a tight leash.

My mother shakes me awake at five a.m. I fumble into my work clothes alongside the others, groggy and half asleep. The five of us try not to wake the littler ones as we tiptoe down the stairs to the utility room, bustle into our jackets, and head out to feed the animals. My belly is heavy with dread. The chores have become a routine, but they haven't gotten any easier, especially with the new electric fence.

Winter isn't helping matters. It seems the sun went south with the geese, abandoning the sky, which is now gray and moody in its absence. The trees, stripped of their leaves, shiver in long rows along the roadside as endless snow falls on them. It is always dark. It is always cold. Hopelessness hangs in the air beneath frigid clouds.

The ground is hard and slippery with snow, and in the sub-zero temperatures, my toes tingle inside my thin rubber boots. I make my way to the corncrib, struggling as I do every day to get the hook out of the eye of the latch on the poorly-hung, battered screen door. Snow drifted into the crib overnight, causing the ears of corn to fuse together in icy clumps that I can't break apart with my hands. When I kick to break them up, pain from my frozen foot explodes inside my boot, and it feels as though my toes have shattered. I am certain if I pull my boot off and tip it upside down, shards of toes will fall out.

The heavy bucket of corn bumps along as I drag it behind me to the fence where the pigs are already lined up, squealing for food. Up close, with their mouths open and their jagged teeth exposed in anticipation, the bristled creatures still frighten me.

And now comes the hard part—getting over the fence without electrocuting myself. I set the bucket on the ground and gingerly lift one leg over the fence, straddling the wire that nearly touches my pants at the crotch. I stretch to my tiptoes, bringing my other leg up and over as the pigs rush at me, impatient for breakfast. One nudges me when I lean back over the fence to retrieve the bucket of corn, pushing me into the electric fence. The shock is intense, and I cry out, scrambling to regain my balance.

The pigs are my enemies—sneaky, distasteful animals. I loathe and distrust them. When I finally get the bucket safely over the fence, I fill the trough as they swarm me, fighting each other for space. I get pinched between two of them, and their massive bodies squeeze me as I try to escape from the feeding frenzy.

It takes me ten minutes to break up the ice in the water trough. I work cautiously, careful not to puncture the trough with the sharp blade of the pickax. Michael recently poked a hole in a water trough and suffered my father's wrath for it. When I bring buckets of water to the pig pen, they crowd around me, squealing loudly in complaint. I throw sharp chunks of ice at them, grinning as they yelp in pain. I hate them. I hate how they mock me with their dark little eyes and push at me with their filthy, wet snouts.

Clumsy in my bulky winter clothing, I electrocute myself again and again as I climb blindly over the fence in the unlit barnyard, the current causing my body to jump and jerk unnaturally.

I get back in the house too late to wash up properly before the school bus arrives, and when I enter my kindergarten class-room, I worry I might smell like pigs. I am grateful for the much-needed diversion school offers. It makes my home life more bearable. School adds a dimension to my narrow world of farm, church, and the rare occasion when I get to accompany my mother to the grocery store. Every day is a new adventure with glue and tiny blunt scissors and crayons and packages of colored construction paper. Everything smells clean and unused. In my activity book, I draw a line from the dog to the bone, from the priest to the church.

Mrs. Walters brings her chair from behind the desk, and we gather on the floor around her for Reading Time. It is my absolute favorite part of the day, and I sit right next to her, soaking in every word. She reads stories of tiny fairies and giants, a cat with big boots. Today we hear about a talking bear that gets lost in a train station. She turns the book around to show us illustrations of a chubby bear in a floppy hat. These vivid stories open doors to new worlds—happy worlds, magical worlds—and I fall earnestly into every one of them. Only during Reading Time do I truly forget about my life at home.

I fight the urge to wrap my arm around my teacher's leg, to lean my head against her knee. If she'd let me do that, and if she kept reading, I think I could close my eyes and stay right here for the rest of my life.

Leslie and I are best friends now, and we sit together on the bus each afternoon on the way home from school. She talks a lot, and giggles, and shares little square candies with me that burst with peanut butter when I bite into them. She says her father is a policeman, and he is married to her stepmother. "My older brother has polio," she confides, satisfying a question I have had about why he walks funny.

I am thrilled Leslie has shared this information about her brother, and I wonder if she will tell me anything else in confidence. Like maybe about her father yelling all the time and hitting her. School is the first chance I've had to be around kids other than my siblings, so I am unsure what kids talk about with each other, what secrets they may share with one another. I sit next to my new friend in anxious anticipation that she will spill some of her secrets, and in doing so allow me to spill some of mine. She chats on and on about her annoying big sister, but offers up nothing further. I assume her family keeps their secrets at home, just like mine does, so I don't tell Leslie anything about my family.

Leslie gets off the bus before me—everyone does. Our house is the last one on the afternoon bus line. At home, I am eager to tell my mother all about what I learned at school today. She is in the living room with Joey suckling from beneath the diaper over her shoulder. I kick my shoes off in the utility room and start talking about the funny bear.

"Not now." She waves me off. "You can tell me about it later. Go change your clothes. Lunch is on the table."

She pulls Joey out from under the diaper, momentarily exposing his head full of thick, black hair. She flips him around and moves the diaper to her other shoulder, then tucks him back under, all in one swift movement, without ever looking at him. I plod up the stairs, my high spirits from school fading with each step, then change out of my dress and join my younger siblings at the kitchen table. Luke and Mary are there, gobbling peanut butter and jelly sandwiches; Simon makes mush of his from his high chair.

"Hurry up and eat. Drink your milk. Then get upstairs for your naps," Mom calls from the living room.

I don't want to take a nap. I'm five now and feel too old for naps. I plead my case to my mother after she lays Joey back in his crib in her room.

"Mrs. Walters already had us put our heads down for rest period. I'm not tired."

Mom wipes the grime off Simon's hands and face with a washcloth. She doesn't respond immediately, which makes me hopeful. Once Simon is in his crib, she orders Luke and Mary upstairs.

"Okay," she says to me. "You can stay downstairs, but you have to lie on the couch with me because *I* need to rest."

The anticipation of time alone with my mother is as sweet as sugar on my tongue. I yearn to feel her arm wrapped around me as we lie together on the couch. I don't even care anymore about sharing the details of my day at school. If she cradles me to her, I will lie still for as long as she wants.

"You in back," she says, and I smush myself against the couch cushions as she lowers her body down next to me. "Hush now. I need some rest."

She faces away from me and falls asleep immediately. In the silence, I study her broad back, listening to her rhythmic breathing. The yearning does not go away. I want to bury myself in the heat radiating from her body, tuck into her, and breathe in her powdery smell. But I hesitate, worried that if I wake her, I will never again get the chance to be so close to her. My hand moves to rest on her shoulder—lightly, lightly. I watch it rise and fall, rise and fall with each breath she takes.

———

Late-spring raindrops pelt the roof overhead. I am in that warm, dreamy place between slumber and consciousness when I open my eyes and realize it is the middle of the night and the warmth is coming from beneath me in a circle of urine that extends halfway up my back.

I lie still, listening to the sounds of rain, until I can no longer stand the stink coming off me. I am ashamed of my bed-wetting even though I have no control over it. Every night, Mom asks me over and over, "Are you sure you don't have to go to the bathroom before bed?" It doesn't matter if I do or don't go; most nights I wake up with a wet bed.

Cool nighttime air rushes over me when I throw the covers back and climb out of the bed, guilt gripping me like large hands tight around my neck. I dread facing my mother in the morning when I haul the soiled sheets downstairs. And how she will scold me for creating more laundry for her—don't I think she has enough to do already without me adding wet bed sheets?

A shiver runs from my neck down to my bare feet as I move through the darkness, peeling off the soiled pajama bottoms clinging to my body. Once I've changed into dry pajamas, I begin the rest of my nightly routine—the part that makes Mom even angrier than the urine-soaked sheets. I dig through the dirty laundry piled high in the hamper, searching out garments that belong to my sisters and me. I am going to use dirty clothes to cover the wet spot. Dirty girl clothes seem cleaner than dirty boy clothes to me, and when I have an armload, I return to my bed and begin the ritual of the three-layer patchwork that will cover every inch of wetness: jeans on the bottom, sweatshirts in the middle, and T-shirts on top. I work methodically, overlapping the garments so no dampness will leak through when I get back into bed.

Mary is too little to care that I'm using her clothes, but in the morning, Kathy will holler at me to stop using hers to cover up my pissy bed, and Lizzy will say it's disgusting and stomp off in tears to tell Mom. I hate doing this to my sisters, and I hate the additional burden I put on my mother every day, but it is the only solution I can think of in the blackness of night. I climb on top of the dry, dirty clothes heap and fall back into a fitful sleep, fretting about all the grief I will get by the light of day.

I wake to find Kathy sitting on her cot with a frown on her face. I think she knows what I've done to her clothes in the night, and I wait for her to start yelling at me. But Kathy isn't looking at me. Her head is cocked—she is listening. And then I hear it too, that familiar sound coming from the kitchen below. The morning has arrived with bigger problems than my wet bed. God has brought my mother another gift.

Joey is barely five months old.

———————

The list of summer projects grows faster than the alfalfa in the fields. Now that school is out, we work from sunup to sundown trying to accomplish them. We finish planting crops in empty fields, build a cinder block barn for more cows, and continue fencing in vast grazing areas for the hundred head of beef cattle we have been gradually acquiring. My father switches back to nights at the factory, and once again he is everywhere, making it difficult to escape the yelling, the kicks, and the punches. We are all fair game for his rages, which appear frequently and without warning, like swift-moving black rainclouds. Thunder booming. Lightning flashing.

Matt is mostly safe, out in the fields on the tractor day in and day out. Lizzy calls our father Daddy and offers to help him with projects before he orders one of us to do so. Her sweet-talking sometimes works to calm him down, and as a result, Lizzy finds herself at the end of his boot less often than the rest of us. I resent her for this, but I feel too prideful to follow her lead. Instead, I just try to stay quiet and out of his way.

Michael has become the favorite target of my father's aggression. I'm not sure why.

Maybe because he spends the most time close to my father, helping him fix equipment. Or because Michael is so like him: hot-headed, short-fused. All I know is that the more my father pounds Michael, the more Michael pounds on the rest of us when my father is not around. It is a vicious cycle of vicious behaviors: Michael hits me; I run to Mom to tell on him; Mom tells my father when he gets home; my father pulls his belt off and orders Michael to the porch. From the living room, I hear the crack of the leather—two, three, six times.

But Michael doesn't learn. His hard shell thickens with each beating he suffers at my father's hands. He is fiery now—a tight bundle of blackness—and flies into rages too big for such a little kid. He no longer laughs, he snorts. He doesn't smile, he scowls.

When he's not lashing out at one of us, Michael is doing other mean things. He tears the small wings off butterflies, saying he wants to see if they can fly with just their larger set. He steals needles from Mom's sewing kit and impales woolly caterpillars as they climb the barn walls, hooting with delight as they twist and turn, trying to break free.

———————

It is early morning. Luke, Mary, and I are on the porch with Michael.

"Check this out." Michael grasps a live daddy longlegs between his thumb and forefinger. He plucks one leg and then another off the spider. The tug and pull launches nausea in my stomach. I groan and plead with him to stop, but Michael smirks and calls me a wuss. "Leave if you don't like it." He pulls off another leg.

"I'm telling Mom," I yell and run into the house. My mother is in the kitchen, and when I tell her what is happening on the porch, she shakes her head and breathes a heavy sigh that makes me feel like *I* am a nuisance. Like *I* have done something wrong. She goes to the window overlooking the porch and raps her knuckles on it.

"Michael. Leave those gol' darn spiders alone." Her voice is flat and noncommittal, and she doesn't stay to see if he does or does not leave them alone.

I return to the porch cautiously, worried my brother will beat on me for telling, but Michael is too engrossed in what he is doing to even look at me. The spider has only two legs left, and he sets it on the floor, where it wobbles as though on faulty stilts and then topples over. Michael claps and grins, grabbing another spider—the porch is loaded with them—and starts pulling its legs off. This time, he removes all eight legs and then sets the body on the windowsill. He does this over and over with spiders he snatches up from the dusty corners of the porch. The gray, legless bodies sit on the sill in a long, quivering row.

I stand, preparing to strip out of my soiled pajamas on another bed-wetting night, when I hear heavy footsteps on the stairs. I jump back onto the soggy mattress, pull up my covers, and pretend to be asleep when my father appears at the top of the staircase. The moon is bright, throwing light across the room. Through the slits of my eyes, I watch his silhouette pass, head stooped beneath the low ceiling. My father rarely comes upstairs, and I wonder at this visit in the dead of the night. He stops at Kathy's cot, bending down to shake her awake.

"What? What's the matter?" Kathy bolts upright. Fear is in her ten-year-old voice.

"I need you to come downstairs." My father's voice is strangely quiet, and I hold my breath, listening to what he says.

"I have to take your mother to the hospital. She didn't make it to the bathroom. There's a mess on the living room floor. I need to you come down and clean it up."

I watch Kathy swing her legs over the side of her cot and close my eyes as they pass by my bed. My heart beats, and my mind is scared, wondering what is going on. I hear the truck back out of the driveway and Kathy moving around downstairs. Water runs in the sink several times. And then there is only silence. I think I'm going to get back up and go through my nightly routine of changing my clothes and piling the dirty laundry on my bed, but the wet spot is warm beneath me, and I fall back asleep.

My parents are still gone in the morning, and I stare down at a large, wet, rust-colored stain on the living room carpet that wasn't there yesterday. It is Saturday, and Kathy is in the kitchen feeding Joey from a bottle. When I ask what happened, she changes the subject, saying she'll let us watch cartoons for a bit before chores if we promise not to tell our father.

My favorite cartoon, *Mighty Mouse*, is just starting as we sprawl on the floor and the couch, loud in our delight. I am in love with *Mighty Mouse*, and I say I want to marry him. Michael snorts, calling me stupid, and says a human can't marry a mouse. Lizzy is nicer. She giggles, adding, "Especially not a cartoon mouse." I don't listen to them as they tease me—I just watch the cute mouse with the big muscles and cape flying around, helping everyone who is in trouble. In my mind, I talk to him: *Do you see me here? I am in trouble too. Can you come rescue me? Will you marry me and take me away?*

Later, my mother sits in the living room nursing Joey beneath the diaper. She is pale and quiet. Not a word is said about what happened or why she went to the hospital. A whole week passes before I realize the morning sounds from the kitchen have ended.

Among the many random tools the Hawkinses left behind was a pickax with an ill-fitted metal head on its long hickory handle. The head fell off every time we used the tool, and when my father could no longer repair it, he removed the head but kept the three-foot solid wood handle to herd the cattle. Cows, I have learned, do not like to follow orders, and a rap on the rump with a wooden haft is much more effective in getting them to obey than shouting and shoving.

My father calls the axe handle The Club, and while he still uses it to herd cattle, it has also become his favorite weapon to use against us. He even has a home for it, a little nook in the Big Barn where it rests when it's not being used. Alive it seems, like a beating heart outside of a body. Until now, we had suffered individually: a random kick with the steel-toed boot, a whack on the back, a thrown shovel. The Club has changed the one-on-one abuse to a collective assault.

Summer is winding down. The crops are in, the hay stacked in the mow, and a cone of wheat piled on the main floor of the Big Barn. This morning we shovel manure out of the new concrete barn, taking our time, leaning on our pitchforks more than we actually use them. My father is home from work and sleeping, but we know he will be out soon, and we talk quietly among ourselves about what his mood will be. We do that now—talk about our father when he's not around. Kathy is the most verbal, openly expressing her hatred for him. I like hearing her talk this way; her words sound powerful when I feel powerless.

"Here he comes," Michael whispers.

We stop talking as we bend our backs to the task. Out of the corner of my eye, I see my father storming across the barnyard and feel the familiar vibration start up inside me.

"Which one of you broke the window in the Front Barn?" He stands in the doorway, hands on hips.

My siblings and I exchange puzzled looks, but no one speaks. All the windows in our barns are cracked or broken, and I already feel like this is another of his traps.

"I asked you a question." His jaw is set, face reddening. "Who broke the window in the Front Barn?"

We shake our heads and shrug. Still, no one answers.

"Get out here. All of you." He turns and stomps across the barnyard. We set our pitchforks against the wall and hurry behind him, exchanging worried looks as we go.

"That window," he points to a small dusty window. Sure enough, a fresh crack runs diagonally across one of the panes. But two others are also cracked in this window, and one pane is completely missing. That's how things are on this farm—equipment breaks, windows break. A cow could have done this, or a rattling wind.

"I want to know *who* broke it, and I want to know *now.*"

My heart is beating against my ribs as he paces in front of us, hands clenched in fists. My siblings and I move closer to one another as though that will protect us. Still, no one answers.

"Nobody wants to admit it? Fine." He stops pacing and glares at each of us: Kathy, Matt, Lizzy, Michael, and me.

"Get in a line," he commands.

I whimper, knowing what's coming. Lizzy reaches to squeeze my hand for comfort.

"Michael, go get The Club," he yells.

The rest of us shuffle and shake as Michael races to fetch the dreaded thing. This is how it goes. My father never retrieves the weapon himself. He always sends one of us to bring the hardwood stick that will be used against us.

"This is your last chance," he warns, gripping The Club in his raised hand.

Kathy makes a brave move. "Maybe it just broke because it's old," she offers.

My father shakes his head, his face going from red to purple.

"It didn't just *break*," he shouts. "Get over here. You'll be first with your smart mouth."

And then the beatings begin. We are forced to stand in line and watch him assault us one by one as he yells, "Was it you? Did you do it?" I shake and whimper with the others as I watch and wait my turn, my body now a mass of jellied fear.

"Bend down and grab your ankles," he bellows, and when I do, he swings The Club with all his might. When it hits, it sounds like the crack of a wooden bat against a ball, lifting me off the ground with the force of the blow. It burns, like someone lit a match to my bottom.

"Did you do it? Huh? Was it you?"

"No!" I cry as snot runs out of my nose and down my lips.

"Get back here! I'm not done," he roars.

I rise from the ground, bend over, and grab my ankles again. The flesh of my buttocks takes the brunt of the impact. I wail with each strike—two, three, four, seven. Each sends me sprawling into the dirt. I struggle to my feet, gasping for air as I hobble stiffly back to my place in line.

By the time my father is done beating us, he is perspiring and breathing hard.

"That'll teach you to tell me the truth." He throws The Club to the ground, wiping his face with his handkerchief in—what? Satisfaction?

We remain in the line, trying to quiet our cries until he releases us with a "get back to work" command. I limp gratefully off to the barns with the others. As always, my fear disappears after the assault, and I am overcome with anger. A bubbling cauldron of rage.

At night, in the safety of the upstairs bedroom, we pull our pajamas down and inspect each other's bottoms. Harsh, white welts rise on either side of long, red divots where the weapon has struck. Kathy talks about how much she hates him, how she wishes something terrible will happen to him.

"Don't say that," Lizzy scolds her. "You don't mean it."

"Yes I do." Kathy shoots back.

I listen to my oldest sister, her face tight, her body rigid, and I think about my own feelings. About the anger I feel toward my father every time he hits me. And I wonder if this anger is really hate. I hate the pigs, but they are just animals. That I might hate my father hadn't occurred to me until this moment.

"I hate him too." The words come out of my mouth before I know it, and I blush when all eyes turn in my direction. But saying these words out loud brings me a sense of lightness, of freedom. I feel powerful, more in control, and I fall asleep fantasizing about all the bad things that could happen to my father. Maybe he'll get chewed up by one of the machines on his assembly line at work. Maybe his truck will slide off the road on the way home.

In the morning, the welts are gone from our bodies, and the bruising has turned a deep blue-black. Several days from now, they will shift to grays and violet hues. We share the evolution of our bruises nightly. Once they fade to a jaundiced yellow, we stop bothering to show them to each other. They are old bruises. They don't hurt, so they don't count.

Summer ends, and I return to school covered in a crusty scab of bitterness. Ready to fight. Not with fists, but with words and actions. Now that I have tasted anger and hate, they burn inside of me like the Eternal Flame candles at church.

My first-grade teacher is Sister Eunice. She is the youngest of the nuns, moon-faced with dark, thick eyebrows, and thick lips, all pinched beneath her habit. She has a soft voice and soft manner. I am unsure whether to trust her hand, light on my shoulder as she greets me at the doorway to the classroom, and ushers me in with the others. I wear the St. Bernadette School uniform now, a gray and red plaid jumper over a white blouse. The jumper is big on me, faded and fraying, like most of my hand-me-downs.

My kindergarten friend, Leslie, transferred to the public school, so she isn't in my class anymore. We still ride the same bus, but she gets off at the public school with her sister, and her limpy-legged brother. She doesn't exactly ignore me now, but more and more she slides into a seat next to another public-school girl, even when I'm waving to the empty one next to me. I feel abandoned by Leslie, but I pretend I don't care, narrowing my eyes at her whenever she looks my way, hoping she feels my anger.

Mom sends a brown paper bag full of suckers to school for my birthday. I go up and down the rows of desks, handing them out to my classmates as they sing Happy Birthday. When I get to the fat girl in the third row, I pull the black licorice sucker out of the bag. She frowns and says she doesn't like the black ones, just as I hoped. I push it into her fat hand, whispering the meanest thing I can think of: "Too bad, hippo." When tears spring to her eyes, I smile a hateful smile, feeling that flame inside of me, hot and powerful.

But something else is happening in my classroom that distracts me from my angry thoughts. Sister Eunice sets a pile of books with shiny blue covers on the front desk of each row, telling students to take one and pass the others back. I am last in my row, and when I reach for my book, I feel a shift inside of me. The flame dims, anger replaced by curiosity. The book is called *Fun with Dick and Jane*. When Sister Eunice instructs us to open the books and write our names on the inside, I take great pains with my lettering, excitement tickling my insides. *My* book. My *first* book. *All* mine. I turn the pages, drinking in the words with a thirst I didn't know I had, surprised and delighted by how many of them I know. When my eyes fall on unfamiliar words, my mind shouts, *I wonder what that means. And that. And that.* We read a few pages of the book each day, taking turns reading out loud. I catch on quickly, pleased to feel my vocabulary expanding. At home, I study our bookcase, which is mostly cluttered with Mom's knickknacks. There are only a few books pressed together on one end of a shelf.

Winter is here, and the sun sets early over our barren fields. My father is working the day shift again and usually comes home in a better mood than when he's here all day. After chores, supper, dishes, and homework, he allows a couple hours of TV before bedtime. My siblings crowd together on the couch and floor in the living room while I sneak away to the attic with *The Bobbsey Twins* tucked under my arm.

The cover of this book shows the main kids—two sets of twins—in a winter scene. I look at them, wondering what it would be like if we had twins in our family. Luke and I are what Mom calls "almost Irish twins" because we were born barely a year apart. But what if we were *real* twins? Would we both have blond hair like me, or would I have dark hair like him? Would we wear matching outfits like the Bobbseys do? And what if my father wore a white shirt and a tie to work like theirs does, and my mother talked to me about interesting things and wore a dress and high heels even when it wasn't Sunday?

I settle cross-legged on the throw rug between the bunk beds, leaning my back against the bottom bunk's mattress. I open the book, shifting my body so the overhead light hits the page. Without even noticing it, everything around me fades: the sound of the television, Mom in the kitchen, the cows mooing in the field. The bunk beds disappear along with the rug I sit on. Even I disappear. I am on the wooden sled with Nan and Bert and Flossie and Freddie. Bert is in front, steering the sled with his feet. My mittens are dry and warm, my arms wrapped around Flossie. Down, down the snow-packed hill we race, cold air turning my cheeks rosy red. We hoot and laugh without a care as this wondrous world, blanketed in white, flies past us.

Books offer but a brief reprieve from the daily drudgery of my life. Up at five o'clock. Wet bed. Wet snouts. Electrocution.

My father keeps thinking up new ways to torment us. We don't have assigned seating at our supper table, so we all try to sit as far as possible from him at the head of the table. Maybe that irks him and that's why he implements the new Rule that involves the chair to his immediate right. Each night, he picks one of us to sit in The Chair and then spends the meal taunting and badgering that person. We try to outsmart him by starting in The Chair, hoping he will switch us with someone else. Sometimes it works, other times it doesn't. He seems to choose randomly, never using our names. He just points that meaty finger—*you, come here*—and whoever it is scurries to the dreaded Chair.

Poor Kathy gets picked a lot. She is a fussy eater and spends more time moving the tasteless food around on her plate than actually eating it. Not that I blame her given how my mother cooks everything in the broiler where flames shoot up around the meat, turning it black and tough. Overcooked pork chops, well-done steak, burned chicken, and then mushy canned Blue Boy vegetables on the side. Salt and pepper are the only seasonings Mom uses: light on the salt, heavy on the pepper.

Whenever it's her turn in The Chair, Kathy says she doesn't like beans, or she is full, and then my father's enormous hand is on the back of her neck, his thumb and index finger pressed into the soft flesh under her ears, pushing her head down, nose to the plate as Kathy chokes on the food and swallows it down with milk.

"Eat every bit of it. Do you hear me? Every bit."

I hate watching this happen to Kathy or any of the others when they end up next to my father, but the truth is that I am grateful when it is one of them and not me. Each night while my father harasses the person in The Chair, the rest of us eat in silence. My mother appears oblivious, busying herself with bringing food to the table and feeding Joey in the highchair.

Tonight, as Mom comes around with grizzled pork chops stuck to a blackened cookie sheet and cut-up potatoes served straight out of the pot, the finger points at me. I move to The Chair, and when Mom returns to serve the vegetables, I look up at her with pleading eyes when I see we are having peas. She knows I hate peas, and he will make me eat them.

I really struggle with peas—I think it's the texture, or maybe that they are gray instead of green and come soggy out of a can. I usually mix them up in my mashed potatoes and eat them that way, but they still make me gag. Sometimes, if I bribe Luke with doing his chores, he lets me sneak my peas onto his plate when my father isn't looking. Or, if I'm in the seat by the rat hole in the wall, I wrap them in my napkin and push them into the hole.

So while my eyes plead with my mother, she is intent on her job, dipping the tablespoon into the peas once, twice, three times, until there is a slimy mound of them on my plate. I narrow my eyes, forcing back the angry words playing in my head that I want to scream at her. She seems unaware, lost in her own thoughts, her own world, as she lifts the pot over my head and moves down the line.

The peas don't blend easily with the meat and chopped potatoes, and my stomach grinds each time I swallow a spoonful of potatoes with a few peas added. I try to include peas with each mouthful of food, but they are chalky and slimy, and as my stomach continues churning, I abandon them altogether. Eventually, my plate is clean except for the pile of gray peas.

"Eat those peas. They're good for what ails you." My father taps my plate with his fork.

"My stomach hurts," I complain. "I don't feel good."

He frowns, then picks up my spoon and fills it with peas.

"I'll help you," he says. "It's just a couple spoons. You can do it."

I shake my head. "I can't," I whine. "Really. I think I'm gonna throw up."

I look to my mother for help, but her head is bent to her own plate, as though she can't hear. In my head, I turn my anger into a hot ball of fire and throw it at her.

"Open up." My father lifts the spoon, forcing it against my lips. When I open my mouth, he shoves it—and the slimy peas—between my teeth. "Close your mouth and chew."

I whimper and gag, trying to keep my mouth closed. The peas go down, but my stomach pushes them back up my throat as I cough and struggle to keep my mouth closed.

"Don't you dare spit them out," he seethes. Face red. Jaw tight.

I swallow the peas again. It feels like a battle is going on in my stomach.

"Open up." He lifts another spoonful.

And then, I get that strange sensation I had on my first day of kindergarten, the sense of everything slowing down. All sounds fade away except his voice, which seems to be coming from the other end of a long, hollow tube. My family fades, too. It is just my father and me and the peas. I open my mouth and watch the spoon move slowly toward me, willing my stomach to calm down as I chew and then swallow the soggy vegetables. But my stomach rejects them again, pushing them back up my throat with a burn. I clamp my lips together, cheeks puffed out, trying to fight them back down. From the other end of the tube, my father screams at me.

"You better not puke those up! Hold them down!" Spittle flies from his lips.

A belch deep inside of me escapes and rushes up my throat, forcing my mouth open, causing me to cough hot, foamy chunks of potatoes, pork chop grizzle, and peas onto my plate. My father leaps up, still in slow motion, and grabs me by the arm, dragging me off The Chair as white spots dance before my eyes. There are no sounds, just him and me as I wait for the kick or the punch. All I want is to get this over with. He pulls me to the corner of the kitchen.

"Stand here and don't move a muscle until I tell you to," he yells.

My stomach roller-coasters, and my mouth tastes as though I have licked rust off a wet tin can. I face the corner and close my eyes, breathing slowly in and out.

My father leads the evening prayer and dismisses my brothers and sisters from the table. I get several sideways glances of pity when they bring their plates and glasses to the sink. He turns in his chair and orders me back to the table, where my mother is clearing the rest of the dishes.

"Leave it, Rose," he says when she reaches for my plate.

Mom protests but quickly gives in to his steely glare and puts the plate back. She stacks the other dishes in the sink, wipes her hands on her apron, and moves quickly out into the living room. Abandoning me. The kitchen feels enormous now with just him and me in it.

I look at my plate where the vomit has congealed into a thick, translucent glob of disgust. My stomach turns over again. I look up at my father. His face is passive now, his hairy-knuckled hands folded under his chin, elbows propped on the table. He speaks slowly and calmly.

"I told you. That you're going to eat this. And that's exactly. What you're going to do."

I will my mind to separate itself from my body. Closing my eyes, I focus on my throat and stomach and envision them detaching from me, becoming just a chute and a vessel to receive. I feel nothing as I begin to eat. I am in my head only, my mind repeating over and over, *I hate you. I hate you. I hate you.* My head feels tight, like my brain is swelling and straining against my skull. *I hate you. I hate you.*

Spoon after spoon. Chute to vessel.

I stay in my head, the words bleeding together now as I'm certain the top of my head is going to blow off. *IhateyouIhateyouIhateyou.*

1966

Waiting to Be Saved

We wait behind the chain-link fence at the edge of the runway, watching planes come and go. My siblings and I are lined up here, our mouths agape in wonder. I wrap my white-knuckled fingers around the mesh wire each time a jet barrels past, shaking the ground beneath my feet, and blowing a hot gust of wind so strong I'm certain it's going to tear me from the fence as the jet shoots off into the sky.

It's April and Gramma Vonglis is on her way to visit, all the way from California. I have never met this Gramma, but I've wondered about her and the magical land of sunshine, palm trees, and movie stars where she lives. Since my father announced the visit two weeks ago, Kathy has led us in a daily countdown to this big day. Upstairs in the attic at night, we talk in hushed tones about how this visit will go. Gramma is planning to stay for a full month. How will my father behave with her here? Will he be able to keep his temper under control for that long?

He paces behind us now, pulling his sleeve back again and again to look at the gold Timex watch on his hairy wrist. We jump around each time a plane lands, asking if that's Gramma's plane. He shakes his head and says, "Nope, it's still a little early." Mom says Gramma's plane will say *American Airlines* on the side, and we peer off into the sky, each of us wanting to be the first to spot it.

"I think this is it," Lizzy shouts, pointing at a plane descending in the distance. We all turn to look, and when my father says she may be right, we squirm and vibrate together in anticipation. Mary and Simon hold their hands to their ears as the plane thunders down the runway. Lizzy pokes me in the arm, pointing at the plane with a smug look on her face. Sure enough, the large letters on the side spell *American Airlines*.

"There she is." My father motions toward a woman who fills the entire doorway as she comes through it. A white scarf is tied in a knot under her chin, a floral muumuu flaps beneath a black raincoat. Gramma takes the steps one at a time, holding the railing carefully as she descends. I wave frantically, even though the sun is in her eyes, and she probably can't see me.

My father ushers us through a gate that opens onto the tarmac. We walk single file behind him, Mom at the tail end with Joey wrapped around her waist like a monkey.

"Ma," my father shouts out. "Over here."

Gramma waves, lumbering slowly toward us in a pendulum-like waddle. She is as tall as she is large, with horn-rimmed glasses straddling a hawkish nose on her broad, jowly face and hair redder than my mother's poking out from beneath the scarf. Lipstick of the same color is painted on her smiling lips. She clutches a black patent leather purse. My father gives her a stiff, one-armed hug as she kisses him on the cheek, but he shakes her off when she tries winding her hand through the crook of his arm.

"Kids, this is your grandmother."

We step forward one at a time to shake Gramma's hand and say, "It's nice to meet you," just as my father has instructed us to. He rattles off our names as we do. My mother moves in last to welcome Gramma.

"And this is Joey." She holds my little brother's hand up in a wave.

Gramma hasn't stopped shaking her head and smiling out of those red-painted lips, saying it's so good to meet all of us, too. Then turns and pats my father on the arm.

"Wow. Nine of them, Ricky?"

My father does his peacock puff, flashing the same grin he does every time someone comments on how many kids he has. At home, Mom sets the table with a jar of sweet pickles and a plate that's piled high with egg salad and tuna fish sandwiches. She calls Gramma *Mom*, although the word seems to stick to her tongue for a second before coming out of her mouth. If the other woman notices, she doesn't let on.

My father is in a good mood and surprises us by saying we can have the afternoon off from work. The air is light and breathable. No fear, no tension. We munch our sandwiches and crunch our pickles while Gramma talks about her flight. After lunch, she settles herself in my father's chair in the living room, beckoning us to gather on the floor around her.

"I brought you all presents from California." She unzips her suitcase, pulling a large cardboard box out and onto her lap.

We lick our lips and fidget. The only time we get presents is at Christmas, and that's because Santa brings them. Gramma opens the box and hands out gifts: mouse ears from Disneyland for the Little Kids, silver cap guns for Matt and Michael. There's a Nancy Drew book for Kathy, a gold metal brush and comb set for Lizzy. I thank her with a blush when Gramma hands me a plastic bag with a tangle of costume jewelry. It doesn't matter to any of us that some of these gifts are scratched or dented, or that the book has a couple pages missing. I dig excitedly through my bag of treasures, and when I find a small turquoise ring, I slide it onto my middle finger, holding my hand out to admire it. It is a perfect fit.

Gramma sleeps upstairs with us in a bed my father brought up here especially for her.

Our three sets of bunk beds had to be squeezed together, and Kathy's cot pushed into a corner to make room for it, but we don't mind. We all like having Gramma up here. She wears a pink nightgown buttoned all the way up to her saggy chin, and she sleeps in late every day. She says it's because of the time difference. Gramma could easily win a snoring contest. I like to stand at the foot of her bed in the morning, watching her sleep. She spills over the mattress, all appendages, like a giant octopus, her red hair fanning across the pillow in a ring of fire.

At school, I brag that my grandmother lives in Los Angeles and is friends with the movie star who plays Endora on *Bewitched*. My classmates are impressed, crowding around me for details. I weave little white lies in with the truth, telling them my Gramma can walk out her back door and right into the Pacific Ocean, and that she plucks oranges off her tree each morning to make fresh juice. Every day, the other first graders want to know more about my California grandmother, and I don't even flinch as I spin my tales.

"She spends her days in Hollywood, drinking coffee with Endora between filming upcoming episodes of the show."

I say the actress's name casually, using her real first name on purpose—Agnes—to give credence to my story. I tease them with the possibility that my grandmother might bring the actress with her the next time she visits. If she does, I say, I'll make sure you get to meet her. Their eyes light up, and I'm a bit surprised at how easy it is to fool them. I never tell them the truth—that my grandmother is not *really* friends with Agnes Moorhead, but merely her personal ironing lady. Or that she has never even met the actress. I can't tell them any of this. I like the newfound attention my stories have given me.

My father keeps his Church Face on when Gramma first arrives, and I hope she will stay forever, but after a week of good behavior, he returns to hitting us when she is in the house helping Mom. Gramma has strong opinions about the tasks my father gives to my siblings and me, and she's not afraid to voice them at the supper table each night. She tells my father it's not right that we spend every spare minute working.

"They're kids, for God's sake, Ricky. They should be playing more."

My father calls our latest project "digging out the basement." It involves shovels, coal buckets, and tunnels. He plans to add three bedrooms to our house: one for him and Mom, one for Kathy and Lizzy, and the other for Mary and me. He wants to put in another bathroom as well, and to do that, he needs to connect the new pipes to our current pipes in the basement. The only way to accomplish this is to tunnel under the living room and break through the current basement wall to tie the plumbing together.

During the school week, we work on the project after evening chores. It's dark and wet under the house, and the place is overrun with fierce-looking black snakes. We don't know if they bite, so we throw stones at them, watching as they slither away into the dark recesses. The buckets are heavy, and once they're filled with dirt and stones, I am unable to lift them. I drag mine out of the tunnel behind me, dumping it on the growing pile in the weeds beyond the house.

Gramma comes down to help us, huffing and puffing with each shovelful. She looks funny in black-buckle barn boots, but I am grateful for her presence and feel less afraid in this space when she's here with us.

"Let's take a rest now," she suggests, searching for a place to sit. She lectures my father again at supper. "It's not right, Ricky. This work isn't suitable for children. It's man's work."

My father shrugs, telling her it *is* children's work, and these are *his* children, not hers. They raise their voices, shouting across the table at each other in a verbal tennis match. Mom stays clear of the arguing, busying herself at the stove. I can't say it out loud, but I feel giddy inside at my grandmother's boldness. I have never seen anyone challenge my father so directly, and Gramma does it in a loud, unafraid way. When they swear at each other, I look sideways at Michael, sitting next to me and biting the insides of his cheeks so he doesn't laugh.

On Saturday night, Gramma offers to help with baths. Mary has joined Luke and me in our weekly bath, sitting between us, giggling as we pile soapsuds on her head. She is pudgy with blue-black hair, and thick, expressive eyebrows. Mom calls her Cookie Nose now because of the freckles that spread across it like melting chocolate chips. Gramma kneels beside the tub, rubbing White Rain shampoo into my hair. She takes her time, working her fingers in gentle circles over my scalp instead of the scratch-scratch my mother does. She asks me questions about school and allows me to babble on and on about Dick and Jane and Spot. My eyes are closed beneath the washcloth I have in place to protect them from the shampoo. In this darkness, I feel wonderfully alone with my grandmother.

After my bath, I snuggle in beside Gramma on the couch—she takes up almost two cushions. Luke and Mary pile in beside me. Mom makes popcorn, and I eat it out of the bowl on Gramma's lap. Her arm is around me the whole time we watch *Flipper*. My siblings and I have worked out a couch rotation while Gramma's here. When *I Dream of Jeannie* comes on, the three of us slip to the floor so Matt and Michael can have their turn.

Gramma says "no thanks" to the offer of joining us on our Sunday excursion to church. She's still snoring in bed when we leave, but when we get back home, she has a stack of pancakes and a bowl of scrambled eggs waiting for us. Coffee is ready for Mom. The butter dish goes around with the syrup, and I eat until I'm holding my belly.

After chores, we head back to the project: coal buckets, shovels, and snakes. The mound of dirt and stone outside grows as we creep further beneath the house. My father joins us, and his endless shouting at us to *move faster* echoes in the tunnel. Tired and worn, we eat supper while Gramma launches once again into her continued criticism of our workload. She didn't come down to help today, but I wonder how much she heard from up here in the house.

"You don't need to be so hard on them, Ricky. They're just kids for Christ's sake."

The downside of Gramma defending us is that my father takes it out on us afterward in the privacy of the barns. Whipped into red-hot rages, he reminds us that *he* is in charge here, *not* our grandmother, *is that clear?* It is. It is crystal clear, and after a while, I stop enjoying the nightly supper table wars.

We keep secrets from Gramma: The Club, the bruises. It is hard to tell what she knows or doesn't know, but the thought of sharing the secrets with her and then having her confront our father is a risk none of us are willing to take.

"Can you imagine what he'd do to us?" Michael asks, wide-eyed behind his Coke-bottle lenses. Yes, we can all imagine, so we remain silent.

Three weeks into her visit, Gramma sees and hears a little more than she should, and she's at him again during supper, standing up when she yells, "Honestly, you're just like your god-damned father." She slams her fork on the table, drawing herself up to her full height. My father stands up too—Gramma is tall, but he is taller. But she doesn't look frightened, and I lean in with the others, fascinated by this woman who dares to defy my father.

"This is *my* house, and *my* kids, and I will do whatever I damn well please with them." His face is purple, hands balled into fists. "And if you don't like it, *Mother*, you can get the hell out."

For two days, Gramma refuses to come downstairs when my father is in the house. Mom makes excuses for her, saying she's not feeling well, and my father plays along, even though his jaw is tight, and his eyes are hard.

We head off to church on Sunday morning, as usual, leaving Gramma snoring in bed. I'm hoping this will be the day when they make amends, that Gramma will have pancakes waiting when we get home, and all will be forgotten. At church, we parade down the center aisle, filing into the first two pews. My father's hair is slicked back, Church Face firmly in place. The priest is in the pulpit blathering on again about sins and guilt.

We arrive home to an empty kitchen and a too-quiet house. In the attic, Gramma's bed is made, but she and her belongings are gone. On the pillow, in her long, scrawled handwriting is a note that says, "I can't stay here another day and watch how you treat your children."

My father doesn't say a word when he hears the news. But later, The Club comes back out into the open and life returns to normal. Upstairs at bedtime, we compare bruises again.

I miss Gramma. I miss her snoring and the squeaking bedsprings. I miss how she made me feel sort of safe. I didn't wet my bed the whole time she was here, and I had hoped to have put that shameful business behind me. But on her first night gone, I am back to it.

I climb out of my soggy sheets and creep across the floor to the dirty laundry hamper, searching in the dark for the jeans, the sweatshirts, and the T-shirts.

―――――――――

We crowd around Bob O'Donnell, all of us staring at the four strange birds in the crate at his feet. They look like overgrown chickens, except they are ugly, with long, pink, naked necks. Two have tan plumage, two are black. They all have matching tufts on their otherwise naked heads, like little hats. Mr. O'Donnell lifts the lid, and they flap out.

"They're called *turkens*." He leans against his truck, chuckling at our reaction to these creatures. "They're a cross between a turkey and a chicken."

I give him a sideways look, unsure if he's joking with us or not. He lights a cigarette with a squint, catches my eye, and smiles. I blush, as I always do, at his handsomeness.

My father has on his Church Face. His shoulders are relaxed, hands buried deep in the pockets of his gray overalls. We stand in the driveway marveling at the birds as they move tentatively across the yard, heading for the spilled corn outside the corncrib.

We have a million questions for Mr. O'Donnell. Where did turkens come from? How do you tell boys from girls? Why do they have that funny hair on their heads? He laughs and answers, openly tickled by our bewilderment. We watch the odd birds, gifts from our neighboring farmer, now pecking at the ground. My father asks if turkens lay edible eggs, and Mr. O'Donnell assures him they do—large brown eggs, and lots of them. Scuffles and squawks over by the corncrib disrupt the moment. We all turn to watch as the geese from Willy Thompson appear, honking furiously at the turkens now scattering in fright. The gander stomps its feet, hissing at the new arrivals, driving them further from the crib.

"That's a mean bird," Mr. O'Donnell turns to my father.

It's true. The geese have been trouble ever since Willy dropped them off, always honking and flapping their wings if you get too close. The gander is as tall as me when it stretches its neck, so I cross to the other side of the driveway when it's around. Matt and Michael are the only ones brave enough to shoo the bird off—jumping up and down and shouting at it—but the gander doesn't scare easily, and sometimes even they have to run when it lowers its head, hissing and chasing them.

"He's just protecting his territory." My father waves his hand dismissively in the air.

Mr. O'Donnell frowns, puts the cigarette to his lips, and inhales. The gander is still honking, marching back and forth even though the turkens have moved way off across the lawn. "Is the goose on a nest right now?" Smoke streams from his nostrils.

"Nah, not yet." My father shrugs. "I'm hoping she will be soon."

Mr. O'Donnell continues frowning, watching the hostile bird. "I'd be careful with the little ones around him." He takes one last drag, then crushes the cigarette beneath his boot heel.

I watch my father's shoulders stiffen, the tiny, almost undetectable tightening of his jaw.

Mr. O'Donnell seems not to notice as he pulls another cigarette from the pack in his pocket. "He's already aggressive," he continues. "I'm just saying he'll get worse when the goose is on her eggs." He strikes a match, inhales, and blows the smoke out the side of his mouth.

"The kids will be fine." My father's Church Face slips. "They just need to stay out of his way. Isn't that right kids?" His eyes are on us, daring us to say otherwise.

I wish I were brave enough to say, "No, we *won't* be fine." I wish I could tell Mr. O'Donnell that it's my father's aggression I fear most. If I could say these things out loud, maybe this nice man would rescue us. *But what if he doesn't believe you?* A voice in my head asks. *What if he doesn't want to get involved? And what would my father do to me after Mr. O'Donnell got back in his truck and left?* My heart thumps in my chest just thinking about it. Gramma Vonglis didn't like what she saw and heard, but she chose to leave rather than save us. Mom is right here, and she sure isn't saving us. *Don't say anything*, the voice whispers. *It's just too risky.*

Summer rain beats against the kitchen window during supper as my father lays out our work plans. The forecast predicts sunshine for the remainder of the week, which means we will be able to get back into the fields. Hay to cut; wheat to harvest; straw to bale.

We eat burned chicken, mashed potatoes, and corn. As my father reviews the growing list of projects, the sump pump kicks on in the basement, and I listen to its hum, hear the familiar gurgling noise it makes when the water is gone but it doesn't shut off. My father bought the pump used, and because the on/off switch is faulty, we often have to run downstairs and unplug the cord to shut it off. My father's face flashes with annoyance at the interruption created by the loud noise from the pump. He tells Matt to go down and unplug it, so my brother scoots off his chair and scampers to the utility room to put his boots on.

"Hurry up," my father shouts over the noise that grows louder when Matt opens the basement door and clomps down the stairs.

I picture my brother down there, working to wiggle the two cords apart. It is a struggle each of us has faced many times when my father, usually from the comfort of his stuffed chair, has sent us down to turn the pump off. The head on the orange extension cord is round and fat and difficult to get a grip on to pull free from the pump's cord. I panic whenever it's my turn, struggling to pull the cords apart as the pump churns in the hole. If it takes me too long, I hear my father screaming from above to *turn that goddamn pump off* as blue sparks shoot out from between the cords. Mostly, I worry I might fall in the hole with the pump and disappear headfirst beneath the water without anyone knowing I am gone.

The gurgling in the basement changes to a high-pitched whirring noise that rattles the floorboards. It sounds like a gigantic beast is wailing in our basement. I lean forward, praying. *Please let him get the cords apart, please let him get them apart.* But still, the noise continues.

"Goddammit, Matt, turn that pump *off!*" My father

stomps the floor with his foot. Everyone stops eating as the sound reaches a deafening pitch. My heart pounds in my chest, yet I dare not cover my ears. *What is taking Matt so long?* My father pushes his chair aside and strides across the kitchen, throwing open the basement door.

"Turn that pump off. So help me God if I have to come down there. Turn it off. *Now!*"

Finally, *finally*, the pump stops, and we are plunged into silence. My thumping heart slows as I exchange worried looks with my siblings about what my father might do to Matt for taking so long. My ear is cocked for the sound of my brother in the basement as my father returns to the table, snarling "finish your supper" to no one in particular. I pick up my fork and fill it with potatoes. Still, no movement from the basement. Matt should be coming up the stairs by now. Minutes pass and Mom finally gets up from the table.

"Matt?" she calls down through the open basement door.

I take a mouthful of potatoes, but all I taste is the metal from the spoon.

"Matt?" her voice is louder now.

Finally, I hear the clunk of my brother's boots crossing the basement floor. And then he is climbing the stairs—slowly, slowly. It seems to be taking him forever. I feel his dread, his hope of delaying my father's wrath.

Mom waits in the open doorway, and when he steps into the kitchen, she gasps and backs away. We all look over and there is Matt, trembling uncontrollably, his eyes so large they look like they might fall out. His mouth has a giant, black ring around it. It opens and closes but no words come out. Mom rushes him over to the sink, saying, "Oh dear, oh dear."

"Richard, you better come look at this," she says as she wipes Matt's mouth with a wet dishcloth.

I strain to see what's happening, but my father is standing now, blocking my view. We squirm in our chairs, trying to get a look at Matt. My father turns and tells us to leave the table and go into the living room. I file out of the room with the others, *dying* to know what is going on. Behind us, my parents speak in low tones. All I can see is the back of my brother's head.

Upstairs in the bedroom that night, Matt tells us what happened in the basement.

"I tried to pull the cords apart, but they wouldn't let go of each other." His voice is quiet and he's talking funny, like the kid on the bus with the lisp.

"I got scared when Dad started screaming so I put the cords in my mouth, thinking I could get 'em apart with my teeth." He looks down at his hands, which are clasped tightly in his lap. "And then it was like I got thrown against the wall, and I couldn't move. Like I was paralyzed, and my eyes were closed, and I realized the cords were still in my mouth."

We move closer to one another on the beds. Lizzy reaches up to rub Matt's back.

"I spit 'em out, and they must've fallen apart because the pump turned off." He raises his eyes, still large and scared, and my insides go all soft and weepy for him. "But I still couldn't move. It was like I was glued to the wall. I didn't know what was happening to me."

We wait for more, but after a long silence, Matt just shakes his head, running his tongue over what is left of his lower lip. Part of it is gone, burned away during the electrocution, leaving a deep black hole that will remain through the summer and into early fall.

———

Dig, dig, dig.

"You've got to make it deeper." My father is bent over, inspecting our work in the tunnel beneath the house. "And wider. I need to be able to move around down here."

When he turns his back to leave, Kathy flips her middle

finger up, and I feel a warm satisfaction spread behind my ribcage at her bravery.

"Asshole," she whispers when he ducks out into the rain and is safely out of earshot.

Ping goes my shovel as it hits yet another large stone. I push my shovel under it and kneel to wiggle the rock out of the ground. Matt is on the other side of the tunnel, swinging a pickax, chipping away at a ledge of shale we've unearthed.

"Watch out," he yells in warning as slivers of rock fly in all directions. Dig, dig, dig. Drag bucket after bucket of dirt to the pile outside that has grown to a small hill. *Ping. Ping.*

Deeper. Wider.

At night I have a recurring nightmare. In it, we are working on the project. Outside on the lawn, a creature creeps toward the opening of the tunnel. It is short and round, all hair and teeth, with arms like Popeye, and long-clawed feet. No eyes or nose, just a face full of pointed teeth. Kathy is emptying a bucket of dirt on the pile, her back to the creature. I stand just outside the tunnel, getting pelted by a hard-falling rain. I try yelling to warn her, but the words won't come out of my mouth. The creature snatches Kathy, gobbling her up until the only thing left is her pale arm, bloodied and dangling from its jaws. Her voice comes from her fingers, screaming for help. She is still alive. I want to run out and rescue her, but I am afraid the creature will eat me, too, so I stay frozen in the doorway, unable to move. Behind me, my brothers and sisters dig and scrape, unaware of what is happening.

Sometimes I wake from this dream with a wet bed and a scream stuck in my throat. Or I wake up trembling in the blackness. Or I wake up when I fall out of bed with a thud that brings Mom running up the stairs. I feel her hand on my shoulder. I sit on the attic floor, crying, my heart pounding in my chest.

"Come on," she whispers. "You're just having a bad dream." Her voice is soothing in my ear. I hear stirring and grumbles from the other beds. "*Ssshhh, shhh, shhh.* Come on now before you wake the other kids. It was just a dream."

Everything is fuzzy, and there's a stench of urine in my nostrils as she helps me slowly up from the floor.

"Oh, Diane, you've wet the bed again." A long sigh. "Go on and change your pajamas."

I strip out of my wet clothes, grateful for the darkness hiding the shame burning on my face as she removes the sheets from my bed. I want to explain the nightmare to her, but she shushes me again.

"Not now. Come on and get back in bed." She straightens the plastic garbage bag on the mattress, the one that is always under my sheet to protect the mattress from getting soaked. "You'll have to sleep on the plastic. Here, let me cover you up."

The dry pajamas are warm, and the plastic crackles beneath me. I close my eyes and listen to my mother descending the stairs.

The nightmare returns, exactly the same, night after night. The creature, the teeth, my sister's arm screaming for help. Mom's frustration grows with each nighttime scream, and after a while, she stops coming upstairs. I sit in the dark on the cold floor feeling frightened and alone.

The wet beds are increasingly frustrating for my mother. Unhappy with my nightly ritual of going through the dirty laundry basket, she scolds me for getting all those clothes *stinking wet.*

"When are you going to stop this?" She yells when I come down in the morning, my arms full of the stinking mess. "Take it to the utility room." She used to end her tirade there, but now, with the dreams and the wet bed every night, she has more to say. "Why are you still wetting your bed? You're almost seven for God's sakes. Only babies wet their beds. Are you a baby? Are you too lazy to get up and go to the bathroom at night?"

On and on she goes, finishing with a warning that she's going to put me back in a diaper, so help her God, if I keep this up. She says all of this in front of my siblings, and I hang my head in embarrassment as they eat breakfast. And while their snickering bothers me, it's Mom's actions that hurt the most. I don't feel physically threatened by my mother, but that heavy sigh, the hands on her hips, and the way she shakes her head and frowns touch me in a place that my father's beatings cannot reach.

Summer ends. School begins, and I wake in the attic to the sound of my mother retching in the kitchen sink below. I listen, silently cursing God and his gifts.

Mrs. Daniels, my second-grade teacher, reads to us from a thick book called *The Bible Story*. In it, two brothers make sacrifices to God, and for reasons that are not explained, God likes one of the sacrifices better than the other. This makes the other brother so jealous that he kills the favored brother, and when he denies it, God gets mad and sends him out to the desert to wander around for the rest of his life. It's an interesting and gruesome story, but I don't get the point. Is it about giving good gifts? Or the evils of jealousy? Or what happens when you make God angry? Mostly, the story just leaves me wondering about this God that I dislike more and more with each meaningless Sunday lecture from the priest and each passing day under my father's tyranny. If He loves us all so much, why does He play favorites with these two brothers? Why doesn't He protect my brothers and sisters and me? And another thing—why does He keep sending babies to my mother?

I fret over this last question all afternoon and for the following three days. At home, I tug on my mother's apron. "If I don't want to have as many babies as you have, is God going to make me?"

She looks down at me for a long minute, blank-faced, and then says, "God will know exactly how many children to give to you." She shakes her head, exasperated. "Why are you worrying about this now? You've got a long time before you have to think about babies."

But I am worried that if I don't speak up now, God will trick me into having too many babies when it's my turn, punishing me like I feel He punishes my mother every time He sends her another one. I don't know what a mother is supposed to feel toward her children, but there is no joy on my mother's face when she deals with us. It all seems to be work to her. I have no memories of ever receiving a kiss or hug from my mother. Not one. No one-on-one time. No questions about school, no interest in homework. It's not just me, it's all of us. Not even the babies get cuddled. Sure, she sits in a chair and holds them while they feed, but she is often either half-asleep or staring out of vacant eyes as they nurse.

1967

Hissing Geese

Michael swaggers across the barnyard with a smirk on his face.

"I got a new word, and it's a really, *really* bad one."

My brother has brought home a bunch of swear words this year, compliments of his third-grade friend Tim Malone. Tim, with his black eyes and shaggy head of dark, untamed hair, is known as one of the "wild" kids, a label he seems to wear proudly.

Michael oozes with self-satisfaction every time he whispers a new swear word, slipping it to me like forbidden candy: *shit, bastard, bitch.* I'm not sure why he shares these words with me, but I am grateful for them, and I tuck them away in my secret sack of other treasured words: *asshole, goddammit, hell,* and *Jesus Christ.* Knowing these words and knowing my father doesn't know I know them makes me feel powerful somehow. I gather them all in my head—an arsenal that booms silently after each of his attacks.

Michael looks around to be sure no one is within earshot. He leans in. "It's *fuck.*"

The word has a hard ring to it, like the thud of the clapper against the giant bell in our church steeple.

"I don't know what it means, but Tim says it's the *worst* word there is. Worse than all the others put together."

I smile back at Michael, the word now delicious on my own tongue: *fuck*.

As we cross the snow-covered driveway headed toward the house, I mumble the word over and over, trying to work out in my brain how to use it in a sentence. My head is bent so I don't see my father coming toward us. Too late, Michael nudges me.

"What did you just say?" My father's eyes are opened in an unusual display of surprise. I take a quick step back, the lump of my heart in my throat.

"I asked you a question. Where did you learn that filthy word?" He moves closer to me, and I turn to Michael, watching his eyes narrow to slits behind his lenses. My father catches the exchange, and his head snaps to the left.

"Did you teach your sister that word?" He advances, grabbing Michael by the shoulders. "I asked you a question." His teeth lock tight around his words.

Michael nods, still looking at me. I hold my breath, readying for the attack as my father's eyes shift from Michael to me and back again. *Will it be The Club? His boot?*

"Stay right there." He lets go of Michael's arm and stalks toward the house. We exchange looks of confusion when my father reappears holding a bar of Ivory soap.

"Open your mouth," he growls. When I do, he pushes his big, hairy-knuckled fingers into it, sawing the soap back and forth across my bottom teeth. I gag on the fingers and the bitter taste of soap, tears stinging at the corners of my eyes.

"Don't you dare spit this out," he warns.

He makes Michael bite a chunk off the bar and then tells us to climb up on the snow pile in the driveway to sit and think about this for a while. He says he never, *ever* wants to hear that filth from either of us again, have we got that? We nod, our soap-filled mouths closed tight.

"And don't you *dare* spit that soap out until I say." He turns and heads back to the house, slamming the porch door on the way in.

Michael and I sit side by side on the snow pile for a long time. My mouth fills with bitter, soapy saliva, and I fight to keep it from sliding down my throat. I want to apologize to my brother, worried he will pound on me later for ratting him out. But when I turn to him, Michael doesn't look at all angry. From behind his Coke-bottle glasses, his eyes gleam with mischief.

"Watch this," he whispers, dipping his mitten into the snow and filling his mouth with it. As he chews the soap and snow, bubbles emerge from between his lips. He blows them into the air, snorting with self-appreciation. I start giggling—I can't help myself—and when he says, "try it," I bring a handful of snow to my own mouth. The bitter taste fades, and soon I have bubbles pouring from my mouth. All these bubbles remind me of *The Lawrence Welk Show*, and I do my best whispered impression: "Somebody turn offa da bubble machina." This cracks Michael up even more. He leans over and very, very quietly says, "Fuck."

I hold my gloved hand in front of my mouth, just in case my father is watching us from the kitchen window. Grinning from behind the safety of the glove, I say it too: "Fuck."

———

School is my safe place, a temporary shelter from all that is happening at home. Here, I feel free to unleash my own pent-up feelings. I tightly pack fury and frustration together, like a snowball, with all those words Michael taught me buried inside like little stones. Then I hurl it in an attack on a classmate who has done nothing to me.

On Valentine's Day, I give the fat girl a card with a hippo on it, waiting and waiting with a smile on my face and hatred in my heart for her to open it. What I don't realize is that while I'm sitting here consumed by this displaced anger, I am missing all the joy around me. The stack of cards on my desk from other students, the cheery well-wishing, the sugary cupcakes with pink frosting and heart candies on top that Brenda's mother sent in. I am jealous of Brenda because her father died when we were in kindergarten.

All during the festivities, I keep my eyes on the fat girl, watching as she opens her cards, anxious for her to finally get to mine. I savor the look as her face falls and tears come to her eyes. And when she looks at me with all that hurt on her face, I mouth the words "Ha-ha you fat fuck," feeling a dark, hot glee of satisfaction spread inside of me.

―――――――

I pause on the porch steps one spring morning, listening to the trumpeting chorus of a flock of Canadian geese returning home, the welcome sound of winter ending. Their honking is deafening as they fly overhead in a V formation. I try counting the dots in the hazy blue-white sky.

I grab my bucket and head to the corncrib to start my chores, the fading sounds of the geese pleasant in my ears. I fumble, as I do every day, to free the latch on the poorly hung door, vaguely aware of movement on the other side of the corncrib. Suddenly, the gander rushes around the corner and starts pecking at my heels. When he lifts his head, we are eye to eye, and I scramble in fear to open the door as I stare into his open, hissing mouth. I make it inside and pull the door closed behind me, my mind muddy, my heart pounding in my chest. I peer through the slats on the side of the corncrib where the goose is busy gathering hay, grass, and twigs. The gander joins her, still honking and stamping his feet.

They are building a nest. Right here. Right next to the corncrib. Icy cold dread moves slowly beneath my skin as I remember Mr. O'Donnell's warning. My hands shake as I fill the bucket with corn, wondering how I will get out of here safely. I tiptoe to the door and whisper, "Please don't see me, please don't see me." When the gander finally moves off, I flee across the barnyard, dragging the heavy bucket behind me.

Later, when I return for evening chores, I approach the corncrib with caution. I hear the honking and flapping of wings before I see the gander racing toward me, hissing, and pecking at the backs of my legs as I try outrunning him.

Each day the bird grows bolder, and every morning and evening, I have a single thought in my head: *If only I can get to the crib before he sees me.* But he is always there, waiting, and he chases me, hissing and biting my fingers and the backs of my legs when he catches me. I stumble into the corncrib, kicking at him as I struggle to pull the door closed against the snake-like neck, the mouth filled with rows of sharp, tiny teeth, heart hammering in my chest. I shout out: *Help! Somebody, help!* But my siblings can't hear me from the barns, and minutes pass by while I cry with fear and frustration, trapped here, waiting for the gander to grow weary and move away.

Days pass, and when the goose starts sitting on her eggs, the gander becomes more protective and more aggressive. Sometimes I don't make it across the driveway before he is after me. If I do get inside the corncrib, he thrusts his neck between the slats, hissing and trying to bite me.

I gather up my courage one morning, telling myself that I am going to chase the gander off the way I've seen Matt do. I cross the driveway with renewed determination, watching as it appears, running at me with its neck out and low to the ground. I raise my hands above my head, waving and shouting, just like Matt does. But the bird keeps coming. He might be afraid of Matt, but he is not afraid of me.

I hadn't considered a full-blown attack. Too late, I stumble backward, startled as the bird flaps its wings, jumps in the air, and pounces on me, knocking me to the ground. And then it is on top of me, so heavy on my chest that I can barely breathe. The sharp, webbed feet stab the flesh of my stomach; the wings rise and fall, beating against my sides. I hold my hands in front of my face to protect it from the beak biting at my head. Grunting and squirming, I finally drag myself out from underneath the animal and run for safety beyond the driveway, trembling, and crying, gulping air to calm myself.

That night, I examine the bite marks on my hands and arms. The welts along my sides from the blows of the wings are already turning to bruises. The long, hard bones buried beneath all those gander feathers have battered me like The Club does. I barely sleep, and when I do, I dream of the hairy creature in the side yard, eating me now instead of Kathy, tearing my flesh with teeth and claws. I awake to yet another wet bed.

The daily attacks continue. It isn't that my siblings are unaware of what is happening to me, but they have their own troubles to deal with. The chickens get lice and Kathy disappears into a cloud of white powder, dusting them one at a time with it; Matt struggles for an hour to free the tractor, which is buried in mud. We are all pressed for time each morning, doing our chores, and then rushing to gobble cereal, wash up, and catch the bus to school.

Mom knows about the attacks. I saw her standing at the kitchen window with a blank look on her face that first morning the gander knocked me to the ground. I had hoped she would say something, do something. When she didn't—when she ignored it—I understood that abuse is abuse in this house and to speak of it is unthinkable, regardless of where it comes from. Still, her silence about the gander attacks leaves me with a profound sense of aloneness that I don't feel when my father lines us all up for a beating.

The gander becomes my obsession. I think about him all the time as I wait for the eggs to hatch. Some mornings, I get to the corn rib undetected. More often, I don't. I try everything to protect myself from his attacks. I throw corn to him; I throw it at him. I swing the bucket around in front of me, and run toward him screaming, hoping to frighten him off. Most mornings, I end up running *away* from him, my heart beating in my ears. I hear him racing up behind me, and the hiss, and the flap of wings as he leaps on my back, tackling me—*oof*—to the ground, claws tangled in my hair. I fight back, arms and legs flailing, trying to shake off the white-feathered beast that pecks, bites, and beats me with its wings.

At supper, I slowly bend over to pick up the napkin I dropped, wincing as pain shoots through me. I am shocked when my mother notices and speaks up.

"That gol' darn gander has been after you again, hasn't he?" She comes around the table and tugs my shirt up and over my head, uncovering the bruises and bites. I draw my shoulders in against the exposure as she examines me. And then, I *do* hear tenderness in her voice.

"Look at this, Richard. Look what that gander did to her." She turns my back toward him as my siblings' eyebrows lift in surprise that Mom is doing something—that she is sticking up for one of us.

She continues, "I told you last week, we have to get rid of that gander. He's dangerous." She stands behind me. The weight of her hands on my shoulders soothes me. I feel something new—a burst of pride toward my mother for this sudden assertiveness.

My father slices off a piece of fatty pork chop, brings it to his mouth, and grinds the meat between his teeth. All the while, his eyes are on me. The silence is suffocating—I am uneasy in the spotlight, nervous about those eyes. I sense that Mom feels it too because her fingers tighten on my shoulders. My father chews and chews, then swallows and leans forward.

"You let a goose do *that* to you?" He points his fork at me. I bow my head, now feeling ashamed, and I try to mumble an explanation. He slams his hand on the table; forks and knives jump into the air.

"This is ridiculous." He leans over his plate, still pointing his fork. "After supper, you're going to go out there and *show* that bird you're not afraid." He stabs another piece of meat, glaring at me, and shoves it into his mouth.

Mom's hands slide off my shoulders. I feel abandoned as she returns to her chair, twisting her fingers in the hem of her apron. I work my arms back into my sleeves, hurrying to hide my failure. I want the kitchen floor to open up and swallow me.

After prayers, my father disappears behind the bathroom curtain. The air is thick with silence. No one speaks. I help clear the dishes from the table, my insides quivering with anticipation. The toilet flushes and he reappears in the kitchen doorway, ordering everyone outside, *now*.

"You too, Rose," he shouts to my mother, who is in the utility room, her pregnant belly pressed against the washing machine as she stuffs laundry into it.

Once outside, he has everyone line up on the lawn under the willow tree on the far side of the driveway—everyone except me. My arm is clamped in his meaty hand.

"Now," he says, tightening his grip on my arm, "you get over there and pick that damn bird up by his neck and throw him to the ground. He needs to learn you *are not* afraid of him."

But I am. I am terrified. Trembling, I move across the lawn toward the corncrib. As though on cue, the gander appears, rushing at me, hissing and honking. I reach blindly, my hands small around the thick, long muscle of his neck. It is like wrestling a python. His orange beak is in my face, and he's pulling free. And then I am on the ground beneath him, screaming, writhing in the dirt, struggling to get away.

Far, far away, I hear my father's voice. "Get that bird off

you! Goddammit, get him off! Wring his neck! Goddammit, do it!"

I reach out again for the neck, but it darts and pecks, and I can't get a grip. The gander bites at my fingers, flaps his wings against my sides. And then my father yells for Matt to get The Club and for Michael to get the gander. I feel my brother pulling the bird off me. I pick myself up off the ground, aware that my entire family's eyes are on me, ashamed they have witnessed my failure. My father screams at me, but his words are muffled by a loud ringing in my ears. I feel dazed as he bears down on me, his face purple, The Club in his hand. He grabs me above the elbow, and I begin to count as I always do during a beating. He swings The Club—*One!*—hitting me with a force that lifts me into the air. I drop to the ground, and he yanks me back to my feet, tightening his grip once again on my arm.

The ringing in my ears stops with this first blow. The world seems to shrink to a pinpoint around me. It is just him and me and The Club, which swings through the air like a baseball bat. At this intimate range, I hear every one of his words.

"I told you."

Two!

"To go get that gander."

Three!

"And I meant it."

Four! Five!

He hits me *Six! Seven! Eight!* times, then flings The Club across the yard. My mind goes dark, and I lay curled on my side in the dirt, whimpering and breathing heavily, my body throbbing. I can't even muster any hate. Instead, I stare at the rows of feet by the willow tree: my siblings' blue and red sneakers, Mom's ankles swollen in her penny loafers.

"All right, the rest of you can go back to the house now." He turns to lead the way, and I feel something inside of me tear wide open as I watch all those feet shuffle past. Eight pairs of sneakers. The penny loafers.

The new baby arrives with all the excitement of a bill in the mail. Another long-haired boy, this one named Mark George. Mark after one of the guys that wrote the Bible, George after Uncle George, my father's brother. We peer at the tiny face hidden in the blanket. It looks like the baby before it, and the one before that.

My mother is pale and unsmiling. She tells Kathy to put the baby in the crib.

My father says he's starving and rubs his stomach in a big circular motion. He grins at my mother and asks what she's making for supper. I watch her flinch, watch her face turn red and her lips curve into a frown.

"Make your own supper," she snaps. "I'm tired. I'm going to bed."

With that, she turns her back and disappears behind her bedroom curtain. Who knew that a house with twelve people in it could grow quiet so quickly and so completely? My father mumbles to Kathy to make us all some grilled cheese sandwiches. The quiet continues throughout the meal, my father at the head of the table with his jaw set. We don't see my mother or our new brother for the rest of the night.

Four days after Mark George comes home, we pile in the car and head to church. Today is about me—I am making my First Holy Communion. I sit squashed between Luke and Michael in my tight, itchy white dress, a hand-me-down from Lizzy. I hate the lace and the stupid veil.

After her unexpected outburst the night the baby came home, Mom returned to her usual self, up in the night with my new brother, half-asleep in the chair in the morning, diaper over her shoulder. There wasn't time to go out and buy me new shoes (white ones per Mrs. Daniels's instructions), and when I join my classmates in the school basement, I scoot to my desk, hoping to hide my black ones underneath. We fidget in our seats, girls in white, boys in black pants, white ironed shirts, and black ties. There is curled hair, braided hair, hair slicked straight back from freckled foreheads—all of us scrubbed clean and shining like new pennies.

Stomachs rumble around the room. The Catholic Church has a strict rule that you're not supposed to have food and drink prior to receiving the body of Christ for the first time. Not even a drop of water.

"You have to be pure on the inside as well as the outside in order to receive Christ," Mrs. Daniels had reminded us every day for a week. And yet, when she asks if anyone ate or drank something this morning, Debbie Kinney's face drains of color and she raises her hand.

"What did you have?" I can see Mrs. Daniels is as stunned as the rest of us, and when Debbie says toast and juice, our teacher shakes her head.

"Well, then, you can't make your First Communion today." It's hard to tell if Mrs. Daniels is angry or sad as she ushers the bawling Debbie out of the room. "Did anyone else eat or drink this morning?" she eyeballs the rest of us.

I have a secret. This morning, I ate a handful of Sugar Pops on purpose to test my theory of the existence of God. I've drawn my own conclusions about the stories, the rules, and the sins that school and church have shoveled down my throat about God. And today, I am going to prove, at least to myself, that it is all nonsense. What kind of God would be okay with my father's behavior at home and then allow him to show up on Sundays with his Church Face on? What kind of God would make my mother have baby after baby when it is clear she is wiped out and doesn't want them? And if God really loves me so much, how can he stand by and do nothing about the abuse? I shake my head with the others, hoping I don't look guilty.

We walk single-file from the school around the block to the church, heel to toe, hands pressed together at our chests, fingers pointing skyward. Veils snap in the breeze. Proud parents, grandparents, aunts, and uncles beam from the left and the right as we make our way down the church's center aisle. I am happy to see Gramma and Grampa Murray here, and I give them a quick wave.

Father Rowan, dressed in his white special-occasion robe, stands on the altar behind the massive tapestry-covered table. He raises the Eucharist and the golden chalice of wine high above his head. I'm hardly paying attention. I'm thinking about the Sugar Pops, about how clever I felt when I grabbed that handful undetected and shoved it in my mouth. The crunch. The sweetness of sin.

Father Rowan comes out from behind the table, motioning for me and my classmates to come forward. Hands pressed together at our chests again, we line up in a row at the kneeler stretched across the front of the altar. Silence descends on all the parishioners behind us in the packed church. A holy hush. The altar boy moves in, holding the gold plate beneath my lifted chin. I close my eyes, as I've been told to do, and stick out my tongue.

"The body of Christ." The priest lays the host on my tongue. "Amen."

I draw my tongue, now balancing the host, back into my mouth. I'm disappointed by how hard and dry the wafer is, like thin, stale bread. I return to my pew and kneel, head bent, feigning prayer, waiting for the threatened retribution from God. But nothing happens, and I gloat at having fooled everyone. The host sticks to the roof of my mouth, so I sneak my index finger inside and scrape it off.

All around me, classmates count down the days until school ends and summer begins. The air is abuzz with impatient anticipation, like a dog waiting to be scratched. There is talk of family vacations, pool parties, and backyard football games. John Collins is headed to his family cottage on Limekiln Lake in the Adirondack Mountains. I seethe with silent jealousy.

My father switches back to the night shift at Gleason's, and except for our Sunday morning excursions to church, we are trapped on the farm with him, never getting a break from the tension he creates. I am on guard from the moment I open my eyes until I collapse into bed at night, exhausted from trying to maneuver around his moods, trying to anticipate his expectations, trying to stay out of his way. A day rarely goes by when he isn't flying off the handle for any little thing that irritates him: we aren't working fast enough; tools aren't organized the way he likes them in the old chest of drawers on the porch; hay bales aren't piled neatly enough in the barn. Everywhere he turns, he finds something we have done wrong. It's a lot like church, where I'm told every week that I am a sinner even though I can't think of one darn thing I've done to offend this God or anyone else.

After church one Sunday, Lizzy, Michael, and I shovel manure, which consists of layers and layers of straw soaked through with urine and waste that piles up endlessly beneath the cows' feet in the barns. We travel back and forth to the manure spreader. I ignore the painful blisters appearing on the inside of my right thumb, thinking instead of John Collins doing the backstroke in Limekiln Lake. When we finally reach the concrete floor, we switch to flat shovels, scraping them along the slippery surface, scooping up sludge that smells of ammonia. Wiggly yellowish maggots live down here, thousands of creepy crawlies. The floor is also covered in round purple shells that encase even more maggots. They're on their way to becoming the barn flies that buzz incessantly in the dusty windows. We whack the maggots with our shovels and stomp on the shells, which crackle under our boots and roll around like tiny wet marbles. I slip in the wetness, sliding across the shells, flailing my arms to keep my balance before falling onto my knees and bare hands. Before I can scramble to my feet, maggots are crawling across my fingers. I beat them off in a violent frenzy that leaves red welts on the backs of my hands.

My father has been on the warpath again all day. We hear him screaming at Kathy and Matt as they work with him. Later, he comes back to the barn to check on us. Dissatisfied with our progress, he releases a fresh torrent of anger.

"I'm going to the house for a while and these stalls had *better* be finished when I come back out." He storms away, wound tight as a drum. We scamper back to our tasks.

I have had to pee for over an hour, but there's no way I'm going to follow him now. I squeeze my hands to my crotch, trying to stop the urge, hoping that once he's in the house, he will stretch out on the couch for a nap—as he often does—so I can sneak in to use the bathroom without disturbing him. I wait and wait, and when it seems enough time has passed, I hurry to the house, my bladder ready to burst. I open the porch door slowly, so it doesn't squeak, then pause statue-still to listen. *Is he asleep yet? If not, will he punish me for leaving my work to use the bathroom?*

I listen harder. It feels *too* quiet. And then I hear the low, angry rumble of my father's voice. He is not asleep. He is very much awake and right on the other side of the wall. Another sound comes—my mother's murmuring voice. I duck, peering under the curtain on the window of the door that leads into the utility room. They appear before me, my father behind my mother, his huge hand gripping the back of her neck. He marches her forward into the utility room. My heart thumps in my chest. Only the door separates us. My father's mouth is pulled back into a sneer, and my mother whimpers. They are both naked, and my mind grapples with the whiteness and the vastness of all that skin. My mother's dimpled buttocks and her heavy, veiny breasts with large nipples like pink buttons. My father's hairiness, which I never knew extended beyond his torso, is thick at the groin. I blink at the sight of his giant penis sticking straight out. Until now, I have only seen tiny penises in my brothers' diapers, and Luke's shriveled, benign one during baths. This thing is different, red and swollen, like an extension of my father's angry self. I hold my breath, praying they won't turn my way and catch me staring from beneath the curtain. My father veers to the right, his hand still clamped on my mother's neck. He reaches up and tears the bathroom curtain aside, then shoves her through the doorway. The curtain falls back into place behind him.

My ears are ringing, my body shaking. I tiptoe back across the porch and let myself out quietly, quietly. Running down the steps, heart battering my ribs, I whisper "oh god oh god oh god oh god" as I race across the lawn and driveway, through the barnyard, and back to the safety of the barn, wanting to get as far away from what I've seen and heard as I can. I don't tell the others what I saw, feeling somehow embarrassed to say it out loud. My mind is spotty with confusion about them being naked. The story of Adam and Eve teaches that nakedness is something to be ashamed of. That it is evil. And this leaves me wondering why my parents would do something that is considered so wrong by the Catholic Church.

But more troubling is my mother. I had never related my father's anger to her. His occasional outbursts of violence in the house are always directed at me and my siblings. I have never seen him raise a hand to her, and even though I don't understand what was going on in the house, my mother looked and sounded afraid. I mull this over as we continue to shovel manure. I wonder: *Does he have a club in the house, too? Does he beat her with it when we're not around? Is this what my father does after beating us? Go in the house and beat Mom?*

Perspiration forms under my armpits, my heart still unsteady in my chest. If this is all true, it wipes away any hope that one day Mom will take us away from here, that she will protect us from him. If she is afraid of him, too, who will save us? A new fear lodges itself deep inside of me, like a giant ball of hot wax, spinning in the pit of my belly. I work silently beside my brother and sister for the rest of the day. And as I process and digest what I heard and saw, two questions keep floating in the back of my seven-year-old mind:

Why were they naked?

And, why did he take her to the bathroom to beat her?

1968

Sins of the Flesh

We are all elbows, legs, and hard-boned hips smashed together. Kathy is the only teenager, but we are all growing, and as we do, the car's back seat shrinks and the spaces between us become more and more confined. At the supper table, Lizzy and I sit side by side, each with one cheek on a plank that spans the narrow area between our chairs. It's a substitute chair for Joey since there isn't enough room for one more chair at the table. He perches between us, legs swinging under the table. His arm bangs into mine each time he lifts his fork to his mouth. In the evenings, several of us squeeze in on the couch, pushing and bickering, all of us packed tightly together like too many teeth on a jawbone.

And we are developing mean streaks. I don't know whether this is because of the space issue or if we are just becoming less tolerant of one another as we get older. Maybe this need to be cruel to each other, to prove we are tough, is simply a result of my father's abuse, a way to release our own anger and pent-up frustration.

When my father is not around, Luke challenges me to a fistfight. I beg off until Mary steps in, tricking me into the backyard where Luke is waiting.

"I'll be the referee," Mary says, standing between us. "On the count of three, start fighting."

She holds her index finger in the air. *One.* Her middle finger rises. *Two.* I don't want to fistfight my brother, and I keep saying this out loud. I watch Mary's hand as her ring finger lifts, and when the blow to the chest comes on *three*, I stumble backward, startled by the force of it. Luke grins and Mary moves between us again, shaking her head at me. She warns me to be ready this time. I look down at my hands, but they refuse to curl into fists.

"I really don't want to do this," I say, but Luke whines that he won't hit me so hard this time, and Mary starts counting again. She barely gets to *three* when my brother's skinny arm shoots out, his fist popping me on the bridge of my nose. I bend over, moaning and holding my hands over my nose as blood seeps between my fingers. I'm shocked by the attack and hurt by my brother's brutality.

"Jesus. Why did you have to hit me so fucking hard?" I plop to the ground, tilt my head back, and pinch my nose to stop the bleeding. My mouth tastes like rusty metal.

"Come on," Luke coaxes. "I'll let you have the first swing this time." He dances from foot to foot like he thinks he's a real boxer. I get off the ground and wipe my nose on my forearm. Luke stops moving, feet firmly planted, and puts his hands behind his back.

"Go on," he teases me. "Take your best shot."

"Hit him." Mary is beside him, like a cheerleader. "Go on—hit him."

But I can't. I'm not built for this kind of fighting, and I'm disturbed by how comfortable they are with it. I walk away hurt, but also a little ashamed and embarrassed. I am older than they are. I want them to look up to me, not think I'm a chicken.

For her part in the meanness, Kathy has given us each a nickname. Some of them are harmless, like Bubba for Matt and Lucky Lukey for Luke. But others are hurtful. She calls Mary Crisco because she has a round little butt. "Get it?" Kathy laughs. "Crisco? Fat in the can?"

Lizzy is Horn Toad because she wrinkles her nose in disgust so often. Michael continues to be Clarence the Cross-Eyed Lion, and Simon is Porky Pig because of his funny, pointy ears. She names Joey Fuzzy Bear because, at three, he already has thick hair on his arms. I become Teeth when my adult front teeth grow in, dwarfing all the others in my mouth by their exaggerated length. I am self-conscious about them and hide them behind closed lips. It's not just the nickname, it's the way she says it. Now instead of "Hey, Diane, come look at this," she says, "Hey, *Teeth*, come look at this." I flinch at the emphasis she puts on that word, hurt by her cruelty.

I wonder if all teenagers point out their siblings' flaws or if my sister is just tired of taking care of us all the time. Kathy carries the burden of adult responsibilities but is not allowed the freedom that is supposed to go along with them. Maybe the name-calling makes her feel like she is in control, like she has authority. I don't know. Whatever her reasons, we all still look up to Kathy. When we are not being singled out, we join her in the taunting and name-calling. I readily take Kathy's lead, standing with her and the others to hurl the victim's nickname like a javelin.

I don't want to use my fists, but that doesn't mean I haven't found my own way to fight, my own way to release anger. Like Kathy, I launch verbal attacks instead of physical ones. She has nicknames, but I go even deeper with the hurt. I get more personal with the insults. To redeem myself in front of Luke and Mary, I make the mistake of teasing Michael by calling him Fish Face.

"Look how his mouth is pinched in at the corners." I laugh, pointing at him. "And how his eyes are all bugged out behind his glasses. He looks just like a fish!"

Luke and Mary laugh, too, which bolsters my sense of their respect so much that I put aside the danger of what I am doing and continue the taunt: *Fish Face, Fish Face.*

Michael gets angry, really angry, and before I know it, he is chasing me around the yard, cursing me. He is a faster runner than I am. Just as he's about to overtake me, I veer suddenly to the right, gathering a renewed burst of energy, and sprint toward the Front Barn.

"Matt! Help! Michael's chasing me!" I scream, realizing too late how foolish this was. Michael catches me in a bear hug in the barn doorway and pins my arms to my sides as we land together with a thud on the burlap bags of grain lined up along the wall. And then he's on top of me, panting, his teeth clenched. His eyes have gone crazy.

"I'm going to *fucking* kill you." He thrusts his fingers against the flesh at my throat, grasping my windpipe between his thumb and forefinger. A spooky calm settles over Michael's face, and now *real* panic rises in me as he pinches my airway closed. I struggle harder, but I can only make tiny choking sounds as my mind screams, *Air! I need Air!*

Michael maintains the steady, chilling gaze. In this moment, I am certain I will die right here, lying on top of a pile of dirty grain sacks in this dusty barn. Miles away, it seems, Mary yells, "Hurry! They're in the barn."

I blink and blink but all I see now are white spots. I stop struggling, close my eyes, and slip into darkness.

I don't know how much time goes by before I become aware of a scuffle, Michael's swearing, and Matt's faraway voice yelling at him to let me go. I hear all of this from beneath my eyelids. When Matt drags Michael off me, my eyes pop open, and I tumble to the floor, gasping for air. Matt has Michael in a headlock, telling him to calm down as Michael thrashes like a wild bull, cursing and trying to twist out of his grip.

"Get out of here," Matt shouts to me. He is older but Michael is stronger. "Hurry!"

I jump up and race past them, holding my neck, shaking and crying with relief. The house feels like the safest place, so I head there and straight into the bathroom. I don't want Mom to know what happened—I'm afraid she will tell my father, and then Michael and I will both get it. My throat burns as though I've swallowed ice cubes. I look in the mirror over the sink, touching the pink marks on my neck with a shaky hand. *What is wrong with all of us? What have we become?* I ask the girl who is reflected.

Sister Joan is tall and thin with a long, handsome face pinched beneath a white starched wimple. Her features are birdlike—narrow and sharp. When angered enough, she has been known to pull boys out into the hall by their ears. I am afraid of her, but I also like her orderliness, her clear rules, and the high expectations she sets for each of her new fourth-grade students. She scrutinizes our handwriting and then makes a special ceremony of passing out pens to the students she deems have graduated from the pencil. I am one of the first to get my very own blue pen, and when she calls my name, I blush and beam as I make my way to the front of the classroom where she holds it out to me. A gift to acknowledge my hard work.

We have spelling bees and write essays. Sister Joan challenges us to think and to express our thoughts, and through her guidance, I am beginning to see that the world is much bigger than just me and my life on the farm. Best of all she reads to us every day, further fueling my love for the subject. She reads "The Lady or the Tiger." Then she calls on us to share which one we think is behind the door at the end of the story and explain our thought process. I am one of the few who thinks it's the Tiger.

She also reads "The Lottery," a story that captivates me and leaves me feeling equally excited and disturbed, a mixture I realize I like. Sister Joan analyzes the story, talking about the hints along the way. She also discusses the story's tone and what she calls the "twist" at the end. She praises the author and calls her brilliant. I nod in enthusiastic agreement.

Sister Joan moves on from short stories to a whole book. Every day after lunch, she places her black horn-rimmed glasses on the end of her hawkish nose, opens a little green book in her palm, and paces back and forth while reading from it. It's a funny book called *The Good Bad Boy*, and it's a story about a Catholic boy who constantly gets into trouble. The boy has a strange name—Pompey—and uses old-fashioned words like "swell" and "dandy." He calls his father *Pop*, and Sister Joan says that's because the book was written more than twenty-five years ago. The things Pompey does are pretty harmless: he feeds castor oil to new members of his club and charges old ladies to trap rats in their cellars. His father talks to him and disciplines him with words instead of boots and clubs. I like the boy even though I'm a bit jealous of him. At night, I fall asleep thinking about him and the story.

Sister Joan reads only a few pages each day, the hem of her black habit swishing along the hardwood floor with each step she takes. We beg for more whenever she closes the book, but she smiles and says, "Tomorrow." And then, it's on to math. I ache with daily anticipation, eager to gobble up my Velveeta cheese sandwich and get back to the classroom to hear the continuation of the story. I think about the book on the bus ride home and while filling the grain trough in the calf barn, my newest job since Luke took over feeding the pigs. When Sister Joan gets to the part in the story where Pompey and his friends form a club, I ask Luke if he wants to start one with me at home. We set a time to meet and sneak out to the front lawn where we sit whispering ideas for our secret password.

Sister Joan stands erect at the front of the classroom as we clamber in and take our seats after lunch. The glasses are on the end of her nose, the book open in her palm. I am excited for the pacing, and the swishing, and the reading. But then I notice that her bushy black eyebrows are creased, and the book in her hand is not *The Good Bad Boy*. She appears lost in thought. Minutes tick by as we settle in, and the room grows quiet. She finally closes the book, placing it face down on her desk, then crosses her arms and leans back, shielding the book from view.

"We won't be reading today. I have something else I need to address." She clears her throat, the crease remaining between her brows. "The state of New York is imposing a new *curriculum* on us." Her brows tighten. "St. Bernadette School is opposed to teaching this . . . this *curriculum* . . . to our students."

The nun peers at us as though she is searching out the one responsible for bringing this unwanted *curriculum* to our school. I look sideways at my friend Barb, who shrugs in response.

"You've probably noticed that your bodies are starting to change." Sister Joan pauses to clear her throat again. "And that with these changes, you might be having . . . *urges*."

Her words bring us collectively to the edges of our seats, the room growing so still that I hear a fly lift off from the windowsill. Sister Joan pushes away from the desk, clasps her hands behind her back, and begins pacing. But it's not the nice swishy kind of pacing—this is more like a march, and for the next several minutes, she issues a confusing list of warnings against what she calls The Sins of the Flesh.

Do not admire your body in the mirror. There is vanity in nakedness, and that is a sin.

Do not touch yourself while undressing. It is a shameful act, and God will be watching.

Do not show your body to others. It is a sin.

Do not let anyone touch your body. It is a sin.

Do not give in to unholy urges when you feel them. It is a terrible sin.

She ends The Lesson there. And then, it's on to math. On the bus ride home, I review the list of sins in my head, unable to make sense of things. *Urges,* I wonder. *What urges?*

I take Sister Joan's cryptic commands literally, struggling to remove my school uniform without touching myself, which is difficult, especially when I get to my underwear. I hook my thumbs inside the waistband and stretch the elastic as far as possible on either side as I step out of them, careful not to touch my skin and commit this new sin. I do look at my body in the mirror, though—I can't help it—and notice the nubs on my chest have grown just a tiny bit. I am startled that the nun knew this, but I'm also relieved that she was wrong about the urges. Whatever they are, I don't feel any. I go about my chores, still pondering The Sins of the Flesh as I spread straw bedding for the calves. I think about my Saturday night baths with Luke and Mary, wondering if that counts as a sin, and if so, why Mom has allowed it for so long.

I head to the Big Barn where Lizzy is milking Bossie. Sister Joan forbade us from talking about it, but I want to ask my sister what she knows about the *curriculum.* Lizzy is singing softly to Bossie, who stands obedient in her stanchion, chewing on fresh hay. There isn't a trace of concern on my sister's face as she milks the cow, and I pause in the doorway, enjoying her clear voice. I envy Lizzy sometimes and how she can take herself out of this world and go into another one. As I am considering whether to interrupt her, Michael bustles in behind me, wearing a giant grin on his face.

"Did you guys get The Lesson today?" he asks in a low voice, glancing around the barn to be sure we are alone.

Lizzy stops singing and leans out from behind Bossie, her eyes narrowed. "We're not supposed to talk about it," she snaps. She makes a *tsk* sound and returns to her milking.

Lizzy might not want to talk about it, but I do. I am surprised to hear they got The Lesson too, and I hope Michael can explain what it was about. Even though I am afraid of Michael most of the time, he has been the source of a lot of valuable information—mostly swear words—and I'm excited at the idea that he might have some answers to this mysterious topic.

"I had The Lesson," I offer as Lizzy pokes her head out again, frowning at me. "I had it, but I still don't know what it was about," I hold my hands up in defense and watch a look pass between my brother and sister. I hate being the youngest in the conversation and having to admit when I don't know something they do. Michael smirks, his eyes still locked with Lizzy's.

"I know what it was about." He puffs up with importance, teasing, testing, and ignoring Lizzy, on her stool, shaking her head at him. Michael licks his lips, but before he can speak, Lizzy jumps up and yells at both of us to get out of the barn. Michael runs off laughing, leaving me and my unanswered questions in the middle of the barnyard.

Two days pass and I'm still thinking about The Lesson, Sister Joan's words repeating in my head. Before her Lesson, I was oblivious to all these sins, but now, I am keenly aware of my body and obsessed with my own buds, sin that it is. My uniform is a thick jumper, so they are not noticeable at school, but at home, I am embarrassed by the way they poke at the front of my thin T-shirt like two Hershey's Kisses hiding there. I study the other girls in my class, dumbstruck that several of them have *real* bumps.

I am also fretting about the upcoming Saturday night bath with my younger siblings. Mary is fine, but all of Sister Joan's talk about our bodies has me feeling uneasy about being naked in the bathtub with Luke. Until now, I've loved our weekly bath, the three of us a bathtub trio since Mary was old enough to hold herself upright. I never gave any thought to stripping down together and wading into the water as Mom swished Mr. Bubble around so we could put bubble beards on our chins and pile clouds of them on our heads. I love bath time, but this new information makes me wonder if nine is too old to be sharing a bathtub with my brother.

Michael shows up in the calf barn with that I-know-something-you-don't-know look on his face.

"It's about *sex*," he blurts. "That's what The Lesson is about."

I stiffen and stop filling the hayrack. We are alone in the barn.

"Do you know what sex is?" He looks absolutely tickled by my expression.

"Umm, no. Not really." *But I do want to know. I do, I do.*

Michael looks behind himself to be sure no one is coming and then leans closer to me. "It's when a man sticks his dink in a lady's hole and pees in it."

I gasp. This is *not* what I'd expected to hear. I don't know what I'd expected, but this is *not* it.

"That's gross." I frown, now skeptical.

"It's true," he rushes on. "Grownups do it, even Mom and Dad. It's how babies are made." His words hang in the air—shocking words that I grapple with in the lengthy silence.

"Who told you?" I demand. "Did Sister Agatha tell you that?" I feel jealous heat rising inside of me at the possibility that Michael's teacher shared this information with his class while mine refused to tell us. But no, it wasn't Sister Agatha. It was his friend, Tim, of course.

"Well, it's still gross." I don't know what else to say. I'm stunned.

"Yeah, but it's true." He gives me a satisfied shrug, then turns and leaves the barn.

I continue my chores, distracted by the surprise, horror, and disgust of what Michael told me, my mind jumping from one puzzling thought to the next.

That's how babies are made? That's what people have to do to bear fruit? That's what Father Rowan is telling everyone at church to do?

And then: *Who would want to do such a gross thing?*
And: *It must hurt getting jabbed by that thing!*
And: *I don't want anybody peeing inside of me.*

I think back to that day on the porch when I peeked under the curtain and couldn't figure out why my parents were naked or what my father did to my mother in the bathroom. I sit on a hay bale, trying to resist the images now playing in my mind: my father throwing The Club on the ground after beating us and then storming off to the house; my mother, up to her elbows in dish soap or changing a diaper, freezing in place when she hears the porch door slam. Begging "Richard, please, no" as he pulls her away from whatever responsibility she is in the middle of—whatever unwanted burden—and drags her behind the curtain to finish off his rage. Like this thing Michael just told me about. Doing this awful thing to her.

I stand and break open the hay bale, aware that my hands are shaking as I refill the hayrack. Once done, I climb out of the calf pen, worrying about my own hole and the day when a man will want to jab his penis inside of it and pee.

"Take those muddy clothes off on the porch," Mom yells from the kitchen, "and pile them next to the washing machine."

I don't know if it's all the extra laundry or the fact that we are late getting in tonight, but Mom is in a bad mood, snapping at us during the meal to hurry up and finish, don't we know it's bath night? My father doesn't apologize that we are late or even acknowledge that our lateness is his fault. Instead, he gets moody, too, giving us cold eyes while tapping his fork on his plate.

"Do what your mother says and finish up."

I gobble up, not thinking about the food but strategizing how to ask my mother if I can take my own bath. Of all the nights for her to be in a rotten mood, why does it have to be tonight?

Kathy leaves the table to get the bath water running, lifting Mark from his high chair and taking him with her. My baby brother spends more time on her hip than on my mother's. If Kathy resents that, she doesn't show it. She is attached to Mark and calls him her Pal. He doesn't have a mean nickname yet, unlike the rest of us. Mom gathers Simon and Joey, and ushers them into the bathroom, working in tandem with Kathy to wash the three boys.

"Diane, Luke, Mary—get ready for your bath," Mom shouts from behind the curtain.

My stomach is in a knot. I want to talk to her before the others get in, so I pull the curtain aside and step into the bathroom. It's steamy and smells clean in here. Joey and Mark are already in their pajamas. Kathy finishes combing their hair and leads them out of the room. Mom is still crouched beside the tub, rinsing shampoo from Simon's head.

"Mom, can I start taking my own bath from now on?" I hear the nervousness in my voice as I stand behind her and watch her fingers scrape at my brother's scalp.

"Why?" she asks without turning around. She pours cups of water over Simon's head, then pulls him from the tub, shouting again for Luke and Mary to get in here and get ready for their bath.

"Because I want some . . ." I pause, feeling a flush rise to my cheeks. "Some privacy."

She wraps Simon in a towel and turns to me with a puzzled look. "Privacy from who?"

Before I can answer, she turns back to the tub, opens the hot water spout, and adds Mr. Bubble, swishing it around with her hand. Luke and Mary appear, pushing past me as they hurry out of their clothes and climb into the tub. I remain in the doorway, fully clothed, stammering and blushing through an explanation.

"From Luke," I say in a low voice. He and Mary are splashing in the water, talking and looking the other way, pretending not to be listening.

Mom stands up, grabs the comb from the edge of the sink, and combs Simon's hair.

"I don't have time for another bath." She sighs, running an angled part down my brother's wet hair. "Now get in the tub."

My stomach continues to churn. "Please, Mom? You don't have to do *anything*. I'll be real fast. I promise. *Pleeease?*" I whine and beg.

She helps Simon into his pajamas, shaking her head, her jaw now set in frustration.

"Oh, for heaven's sake, Diane, you've got nothing to see. Now stop your bellyaching and get in that tub."

Her words scald me. And like the striking of a match, I am filled with a flame of hate. Hate for her lack of understanding and her unloving hardness. Hate for her dismissal of my needs. I want to use the swear words Michael taught me. I want to shout at her: *It's not my fucking fault that you let your husband pee in you. It's not my fault you have all these goddamn kids that cause you so much work.*

I am almost in tears as I remove my clothes, my face burning with shame as Luke watches, wolf-faced.

My mother leaves the room with Simon in tow, pulling the curtain closed behind her as I slink into the tub, sinking up to my neck in bubbles as quickly as I can. But not before Luke points a mocking finger at me.

"I see your boobies! I see your boobies!"

"You have a hole in your uniform." Connie stands behind me in line, pointing. I know she's not trying to be mean, but I hate her anyway for saying it, for noticing the hole. Perfect Connie, whose mother made personalized heart-shaped Valentine cookies for everyone in our class, our names spelled with red frosting in neat cursive letters. Connie, who has wispy white-blond hair and didn't show up for First Communion in the standard veil but instead wore one with a six-point crown on top, making her look more like a princess than a repentant sinner.

It's not like I wasn't aware of the hole back there. The uniform is a hand-me-down from Lizzy, who got it from Kathy, who got it from who-knows-who. My clothing can be traced back in this way, like generations of ancestors. The jumper was already fraying in that spot at the beginning of the school year, red and gray threads pulling slowly away from each other.

"Be careful with this," Mom had said, running her thumb over the worn fabric. "I just need to get one more year out of it."

And with that statement, the burden to "get one more year out of it" was placed on me. The thing doesn't even fit properly and hangs on me like a plaid sack. Safety pins hold the hem up in places where the red stitching has unraveled. The pins don't bother me because they are mostly hidden, tiny silver lines like hyphens along the hem.

The hole is a different story, something to keep concealed, like a wart. It is glaring, embarrassing evidence of my family's financial status. And until Connie points at it, I have managed to keep this shameful secret hidden, out of sight. I've told Mom twice about the hole, asking please, please, can we fix it. But my mother is not great with needles and thread, and she keeps putting me off. Besides, she is inundated with other demands: changing diapers, cooking meals, washing endless piles of laundry.

"Oh, Diane," she said last week, exasperated at my pleading. "It's not that bad."

But it *is* that bad, and as the hole has grown, it has been more and more difficult to hide. And now Connie is behind me as we shuffle back into the building after recess, looking at the hole, at my secret, and I am paralyzed with mortification. I bow my head against the burning redness on my face, staring back there with her, down at the place where my cotton underpants are clearly visible through the opening. I want to either run away or punch Connie. She and I are frozen here, staring at this hole in my jumper, this portal into my other life, the one I try to leave behind when I climb the school bus steps each morning. I decide I must protect my secret, so I straighten up and hear the lie slip effortlessly out of my mouth.

"Yeah, I know," I tell her. "I ripped it on the slide."

And then I shrug, hoping to look bored and casual, hoping to convey to Connie that the hole is a trivial matter, a small nuisance to be dealt with later. She doesn't look convinced and is still looking at the hole as we enter the classroom. I am grateful to get back to my seat, the secret now safely out of sight. I dare not look in Connie's direction, certain that if I do, she will be pointing at me and whispering to Brenda in the seat behind her, "Diane Vonglis has a hole in her uniform because she is poor."

At home after supper, I bring my uniform downstairs to show my mother. She purses her lips, holding the jumper out in front of her, scrutinizing the hole. I want to scream at her for letting it get this bad, but we have been conditioned not to speak our thoughts or express our feelings at home, so mine are always clanging around inside of me like a handful of nails tossed in a dryer and set to tumble.

"Hmm," she says finally. "This hole is too big to sew. I'll have to put a patch on it."

She breathes out a burdened sigh, the one that asks why I am bothering her with my little problems when she has mountains of her own, the sigh that tells me I just added one more hardship to her already hard life. My mother never has time for my needs. Like when I ask her to test me on my weekly vocabulary words (she has Kathy do it), or when I wanted her to listen to the *whole* story about getting my first pen (*Later, Diane. I'm busy now*). Her sighs used to soften me up inside with compassion for this poor woman who is run ragged from sunup to sundown. I used to feel guilty and selfish, but that was before I was recently allowed to go over to my friend Barb's house after school. Barb's father is also a farmer, a dairy farmer who is well-respected in our town. I suppose that's why my father let me go. And it was there at Barb's house that I watched a mother interacting with her children, asking about their day, and *listening* to the whole story. There, Barb's mother lounged on the couch smoking a cigarette while spinning the dial on the Twister board. "Right hand, red," she called, laughing as Barb and I stretched and contorted on the plastic mat.

At Barb's, I learned that other farms have hired hands, grown men who do the same work expected of me and my siblings at home, and that other kids aren't knocked off their chairs for spilling their milk. (Barb's brother did and he wasn't.) Isolation had kept me ignorant until that day at Barb's, when the realization that what happens at my house might not be *normal* hit me like a shovel to the face. The visit shone a spotlight of truth on my parents' flaws, and afterward, I began observing other parents with their children at church and school, noting their tiny gestures—bending to button a coat, holding small cheeks in their warm hands, kissing foreheads, engaging with them—all of which further cemented my hatred for my father. It also opened my eyes to what a mother is supposed to be, and in the process, hardened my heart toward mine. And so today, I do not feel sorry for my mother. I resent her martyrish sighs, and I resent biting my tongue to keep from saying what I really think and feel as she pulls her sewing basket from a cupboard and rummages around in the bottom of it.

"What if you write a note to Sister Joan that I'm going to wear a dress to school until you can get me a new uniform?" I ask, following her to the table.

Mom frowns over her glasses. "You know we don't have money for that, Diane."

She spreads the patches out on the counter, thick, coarse swatches in various sizes and colors. I know what comes next.

She will tell me to choose whatever color patch I want. To her, this is just like any other hole that needs mending, like the threadbare knees in a pair of work jeans or a tear in my farm jacket. Shabby clothing in need of patches is just one of the many problems here. Our barn boots are also wearing thin—holes in the toes, holes in the soles—and although I wear heavy wool socks, snow still gets inside, freezing my toes and feet. Mom gives us used plastic Wonder Bread bags to wear inside our boots as protection. I pull my barn socks on, slide my feet into the plastic bags, and then carefully pull on my boots. That usually works for chores. But when I'm outside all day, the bags tear and water gets in. Sometimes, when there aren't enough bread bags to go around, Mom inspects our boots to see whose are the worst and divvies out the bags accordingly.

But patches and Wonder Bread bags are supposed to be for our *home* clothing, our work clothes that nobody outside of the family sees. They are supposed to be like my father's rages, and my bruises—things to be kept secret, way out here on the farm, miles from the prying eyes of teachers and classmates. A patch on my uniform will confirm what Connie already suspects, and I feel a hot lava-like anger bubble inside of me at the anticipation of that humiliation. I want to throw the jumper on the floor and stomp on it. I want to curse at my mother and shout that I am embarrassed. *Embarrassed, goddammit, don't you understand?*

"How about this?" Mom pulls me out of my reverie, either oblivious to or ignoring my body language. She picks a gray patch from the pile. "How about I put the patch on the inside?"

She positions the patch inside the jumper and pulls the gaping hole in on both sides. It doesn't look great, but it is a much better option than having it on the outside. I nod and give her a small smile of gratitude as the lava begins cooling. My relationship with my mother is this way now: one minute I hate her, and the next it feels like she really is trying.

1969

War & Peace

"**B**ombs away," Barb whispers, peering at me from under her left arm.

"Kiss your ass goodbye," I whisper, peering back at her. Barb tries muffling her snort, but Sister Joan hears it and stalks over, giving her a whack on the head.

We sit cross-legged, our backs against the wall, bent forward at the waist with arms folded over our heads, holding the bomb drill pose as the town siren wails. The drills have been coming more frequently. Not that I mind—I'd rather be out here in the hall with my hands over my head than inside doing math.

"Why do they make us come out into the hall to die instead of just staying in our classrooms?" I ask Barb when Sister Joan moves out of hearing distance.

"Maybe so when we blow up, all our body parts will be in one place." Barb nudges me with her knee, lifting her elbow so she can see me better. "It'll make cleanup easier."

I think the drills are stupid. The threat of a bomb dropping on our school doesn't seem real to me. The possibility of war with the Soviet Union doesn't seem real. Even the actual war going on in Vietnam doesn't seem real. I don't know anybody who's in it, and Vietnam is so far away it might as well be on another planet. I watch President Nixon on TV, always sweating and angry-looking, talking about getting America out of this war, but even he isn't that real to me in his White House in some distant state.

Here is what's real to me: my father, sweaty and angry in the barnyard yesterday, screaming that he wants to know *who* moved the turken eggs and he wants to know *now*. That was real to me. And lining up with my siblings for the beating when no one admitted they moved the eggs. That was real to me. Today's stinging bruises? Those are real to me. Fuck the Vietnam War—my brothers and sisters and I are fighting our own war. But of course nobody knows that.

Even Father Farrell, the latest priest to head up our parish, is engaged in the war conversation. Father Rowan left our church not long after my First Communion in second grade, disappearing without warning into the night, it seemed. And then Father Leonard, and Father Seamus after him, both shipped off to who-knows-where. The new priest is friends with some bigwig music composer named Alec Wilder, and after the bomb drill, they show up to talk about the war. We stand as they enter, reciting the mandatory singsong greeting all guests receive: "Good morning, Father Farrell. Good morning, Mr. Wilder. God bless you."

The priest says "good morning" back and tells us we can be seated. The composer is handsome, like a movie star with black hair combed straight back from his high forehead, thick-lashed eyes beneath expressive eyebrows, and a well-trimmed mustache. He tells us he is writing a song about the Vietnam War and about peace, and he would like our help.

"I've got the music written already. I'm hoping you will write the words."

This gets our attention. A famous person coming to this little town asking kids for their help? To write a song? I join the wave of excitement buzzing through my classroom. Mr. Wilder ambles up and down the aisles, handing out crisp sheets of paper with the words "Children's Plea for Peace" typed across the top. He tells us he loves how kids think and talk. *Their innocence.* And he tells us that he feels his song would be more meaningful if the lyrics were written by kids.

"I'll read everything you write and choose the best ones for the song. If yours gets picked, you'll get your name in the paper, too. Think of it as a contest."

At the blackboard, in large, block letters, he writes, *WAR IS* and *PEACE IS*.

"I want you to think about what war means to you, or peace, and write it down. Just a sentence or two—it doesn't need to rhyme." He sets the chalk back in the tray and rubs the dust off his fingers. "Any questions?" He waits, smiling as his dark eyes survey the room. When no one raises their hand, he continues. "Okay then. Father Farrell will get your papers to me, and I'll let you know soon who the winners are." He gives a short bow and wishes us luck before following the priest out of the room, closing the door softly behind them.

"Well, this is certainly a treat!" Sister Joan is also excited. "I'll give you half an hour to write down your thoughts. Take your time. Relax and really think about what you want to say."

I write the words "Peace Is" on my paper using my best penmanship, wondering about the prospects of winning. All around the room, my classmates are bent over their desks, most already scrawling away. I stare at the two words: *Peace Is.* When nothing comes, I close my eyes to focus. *Peace Is.* My mind is blank. The classroom clock ticks loudly; I count forty ticks, and still nothing comes to me. I open my eyes and tap my pen lightly against my teeth.

Come on, I scold myself. *You can do this.* I furrow my brow and concentrate: *Peace Is.*

Peace Is. Peace Is. But the clock ticks on and still no words come. I draw two lines through the words and write below them, "War Is." In my head, I am back in the barnyard and my father is screaming for Michael to go get The Club. I am blubbering next to Mary in our line next to the Front Barn.

War Is.

There in the barnyard, I step forward when it is my turn, bending to grab my ankles. He swings The Club, and I feel the familiar *oomph* of being lifted off the ground from the impact. And then the burn of the blow, and my father yelling at me to *get back here, we're not done.*

War is.

I try to shut all this out and focus on the war the composer wants me to write about. I *know* I can do this; I *know* I can. Papers rustle around me. I hear pens and pencils being set down on desktops and students fidgeting in their seats. I sneak a peek. Connie looks satisfied. My palms are sweaty, and my body rigid with anxiety. Still, nothing comes.

War is. War is.

"Time's up," Sister Joan says. "Finish your thoughts and pass your papers forward."

I look at my blank paper, my face hot with embarrassment. There are murmurs of contentment around me when Sister Joan asks how it went. Papers from behind me are being passed overhead, and now I hate the composer with his expressive eyebrows and his fame, hate his stupid contest and the stupid topic. I slip my paper into the middle of the pile.

A week later, the composer reappears. He has chosen the best work, and someone in our class won with an entry about peace. This announcement causes everyone who wrote about peace to sit taller in their chairs.

"All entries were terrific," the man insists, seeing the slumped shoulders of those who obviously wrote about war. "And frankly, I had a hard time choosing."

He thanks us again for our contributions, talks about lyrics and how simpler is often best, how fewer words can have more impact. And then, with a flourish, he pulls a folded sheet of paper from his shirt pocket.

"I'm going to read the winning entry, and when I do, I want the writer to come forward."

All these held breaths, all this build-up. *Fuck this*, I think.

"Listen to what this student did with just nine words." The composer clears his throat and opens the paper. "Peace is a horse with a nose of velvet."

I strain to see who will rise from their desk. I'm betting on Julie because she's the smartest one in our class, but Brenda stands instead. Brenda is a blusher like me, and she heads up the aisle crimson-faced.

"Give this young lady a round of applause," the man says, making a stupid bow to Brenda.

I clap with the others, but I am overcome with a strange sensation that everyone is fading around me and I am sitting here in my own world, away from the grinning faces and the clapping hands. Away from the nine words. From my world, this place of aloneness, I seethe and scoff. *That's it? That's the winning entry?* And within the space of two breaths, I feel the now-familiar flame ignite inside of me, that quick *whoosh* from spark to wildfire in an instant, burning so hot it leaves me bitter and brittle. *Who*, I wonder, *honestly gives a fuck about a horse or its nose?*

I slurp through Sunday's spaghetti supper, wiping my plate with a slice of Wonder Bread slathered in butter. This is one of my favorite meals, the sauce thick with crumbled hamburger.

I fold the bread, laden with the oily red stuff, and push it into my mouth.

My toes are still numb and hard from being outside in the cold all day. I tap them lightly against the chair leg, trying to get the feeling back into them. Thawing frozen toes takes time and patience. When I forget this and hurry to get beyond the throbbing and the itching, I tap too hard, causing an explosion of pain that feels as though my toes have blown apart inside my sock.

Kathy is in The Chair next to my father tonight. From the other end of the table, I feel somewhat safe. I am in a sleepy, hazy daze, ready to get the dishes done, and head off to bed.

Tap, tap. My toes begin tingling. I slowly wiggle them back and forth.

My father leans back in his chair, rubs his hands together, and turns to my mother.

"How about you bring those prunes out for dessert?" he says.

I look at my mother in alarm. *The prunes? He wants us to eat the prunes? The ones in the dusty, dented can someone gave us to feed to our pigs? How did they get in our cupboard?*

"I don't know, Richard." Mom frowns, shaking her head. "I'm just not sure those prunes are okay."

"Oh, they're fine." He waves a dismissive hand. "I think the kids are gonna *love* 'em."

"I don't know," she says again but gets up from her chair anyway. The can is so severely dented that my father struggles with the can opener to get the lid off, but once he does, he spears a prune with his fork and pulls it from its slimy, muddy-looking juices, holding it up dripping and glistening in the air.

"Oh, yeah, the prunes. I forgot about them," Luke smiles. He turns and nudges me. "I thought you fed them to the pigs?"

"I thought *you* did." I nudge back.

"What are prunes?" Mary asks.

"They're like big raisins." Luke puffs up with importance.

"They *are* like big raisins." My father smiles. "I didn't want to waste them on the pigs."

He sets his fork with the speared prune on his plate, hands the can to Kathy, and tells her to take one and pass it around. Kathy wrinkles her nose over the can and sniffs.

"Yuck. They smell bad. I think I'll pass," she says and hands the can to Michael.

My father reaches over and puts the can back in front of Kathy. "I said take one."

His tone shifts the air in the room, causing me to feel a chill, as I often do in these moments, as though the temperature has dropped several degrees in the kitchen. My toes are itching like crazy under the table, but I dare not reach to scratch them.

"You can't be serious," Kathy retorts in exasperation. "These things are rotten. We can't eat them. Here, smell." She tilts the can toward my father.

The rest of us hold our breath, all eyes on Kathy. She is our compass, our leader. More and more, my sister speaks her mind, always with a logic that seems hard to refute. Bold and brave, she flushes now with her own anger. But my father's face is redder, and I tremble with anxiety watching the two of them. He snatches up Kathy's spoon, dips it into the can, and scoops first one and then another prune onto her plate.

"Oh, I am very serious," he spits. "And for that smart mouth of yours, you will eat two."

The sound of the spoon clanging onto the plate echoes in absolute silence.

Michael takes a prune next, sniffing it as he does. His nose crinkles, but he says nothing. Around the table the can comes. Lizzy helps Joey fish a prune as big as his fist out of the can. I smell the prunes before the can reaches me—heavy and metallic, like wet rust. The shriveled prunes are submerged beneath liquid as murky and gray as dirty dishwater. Kathy is right—of course she is. Nausea rises in my throat as I look over at my mother, who is now turned away from the table, fussing with Mark in his high chair. She wipes his hands and face with a wet washcloth, conveniently distracted. And once again, I hate her.

Luke takes two prunes, still believing these are just big raisins. He cuts into the first one, beaming at my father's nod of approval. But as he pops a large slice into his mouth and begins chewing, the smile falters. As he chews more, it turns to a grimace.

"It doesn't taste like a raisin." Bits of the black thing speckle his teeth.

The rest of us stall, pushing the foul things around on our plates until my father says he's done with the dillydallying, and we better all eat up *now*. I cut my prune into four pieces, gagging the first two down with the little bit of milk I have left in my glass. Around the table, my siblings make faces and noises as they, too, struggle to ingest the prunes. Matt coughs, his face turning red, cheeks puffed out as he struggles to hold his mouth closed. *Cough. Cough.* He looks like he's gasping for air. *Cough. Cough.* And suddenly spaghetti is pouring out of his nose, long strands of it, still red with sauce. Eyes wide in bewilderment, Matt finally opens his mouth, letting loose a deep-bellied belch as more spaghetti, covered in meat sauce and prune chunks, spills onto his plate. And then it's pandemonium as Mom pulls Matt's chair out, yelling at him to get to the bathroom, and now Lizzy is choking, and my father is bellowing at her, "Stop that now. Close your mouth and swallow."

With Matt and Mom gone, the room falls quiet again except for Lizzy, who breathes noisily through her nose, sniveling and chewing the last of what is in her mouth. The clock ticks as we wait for Mom to return to the table and announce the obvious—that the prunes are bad, and we don't need to finish eating them. I know my siblings are thinking the same thing because nobody is eating. But Mom doesn't come back, and my father isn't quite done.

"Not one of you will leave this table until your prunes are gone." He points the fork with the speared prune at us, a prune he will not eat. "And I don't want to see *anyone* else getting sick. *Have you got that?*"

Itchy toes forgotten, I chew the last of my prune, rubbery and putrid, upending my milk glass, hoping the last precious drops will help it slide down my throat.

———

I wake in the night to groans and gagging all around me. In the dim light, I see Kathy bent over Joey's bed. He is crying and vomiting down the front of his pajamas. Everyone else is in a jumble, running toward the stairwell. I feel vomit rising in my own throat and jolt out of bed, bumping into Luke as I hurry to the stairs. Michael is in front of me, dashing headlong down the stairway, a pile of vomit trailing him. In the chaos and panic, Mom bursts through her bedroom curtain, pulling her housecoat around her.

"Cover your mouths!" she shouts. "Cover your mouths!"

I put one hand over my mouth, holding the rail with the other as I swoop down the staircase, vomit rushing up my throat. Too late, I realize I won't make it to the bathroom. It shoots from between my lips as I grip the railing with both hands, steadying myself against the onslaught as violent waves of nausea rip through me. Mary is on the landing now with her little hand across her open mouth as vomit pours from between her fingers.

Mom screams, "Stop! Just stand still!" But it's too late— the stairs are covered in vomit, and there are trails leading through the living room to the bathroom. Behind the bathroom curtain, I find Matt and Lizzy hunched over the toilet shoulder to shoulder, and Michael hacking into the sink. Kathy rushes in holding Joey in her arms, dark stains covering his footed pajamas. The ordeal keeps us up most of the night, the little ones frightened and crying. Lizzy and I help them into dry pajamas, trying to comfort them while Mom and Kathy strip soiled sheets from our beds.

My father does not stir from his bed during any of this. In the morning, he is gone to work, and Mom is on her hands and knees with a bucket of soapy water and a rag, mopping up the stairs. We are shaky and weary with exhaustion. Luke can't even get out of bed. I feel lightheaded as I go about my chores. At breakfast, Mom places the back of her hand on each of our pasty foreheads, deciding who is well enough to go to school. We don't talk about what happened last night.

"Where are the rest of the kids?" our bus driver asks when just Matt, Michael, and me board the bus. Matt says they are all sick, nothing more.

I gaze out the window on the long ride into town: at the snowy fields, at smoke billowing from chimneys, and mothers in driveways kissing their children as they board the bus. My stomach lurches at each stop, so I close my eyes, pressing my forehead to the cool glass, not paying attention to kids filtering down the aisle, filling the seats around me. I think about last night, about the prunes, and about how they were meant for the pigs. And I think that my father did this on purpose. I'm not angry; I am too wiped out to feel such a strong emotion, but I am deeply disturbed by the idea that he knew the prunes were bad and fed them to us anyway. *What if they had been more poisonous? What if they hadn't just made us sick? What if they had killed one of us? What then?*

I turn my head, resting my right cheek on the cold window—it soothes me—and I wonder if I really am well enough to go to school today. I wish there was someone I could talk to about what happened last night, someone I could trust not to tell my father. I shudder at the thought of what he would do if he found out I was telling our secrets. And yet something nags at me as the bus bumps along, a voice in my head telling me this is a rare opportunity because with only three Vonglis kids going to school, I have hard evidence. *Maybe*, that voice says, *there is a way to tell someone why there are only three of us*, a roundabout way that will make that person ask *me* questions instead of me having to tell them outright.

What about Mrs. Cook, the school nurse? I think she might listen. Or Sister Joan? My teacher knows me better than the nurse does, and she is so smart she will figure it out. I will only have to hint at what happened, and she will be on it. I picture her taking me by the hand down to the nurse's office and closing the door so the three of us have privacy. They will sit with me and ask me to tell them all about it. Will I be too frightened, or will I be brave? Will I tell them just about last night or will all the other secrets pour out of me? I picture the two of them leaning forward in their chairs with grave, concerned faces and me crying as the words spill from my mouth, feeling relief at placing all this information safely in the women's capable hands. I see Sister Joan rise to her fullest height, telling me to stay here with the nurse because she is going to call the police and then this nightmare will be over, do I understand? *Over*. Her hand feels warm on my shoulder.

I think about the police walking onto the factory floor and handcuffing my father in front of his coworkers. And then I picture my siblings gathered around me at home later, slapping me on the back and thanking me for my bravery, for speaking up and saving us all.

But then, a different voice, the quiet, nervous one in my head, asks, *What if they don't believe me, and they tell my father what I told them?* This is the voice that usually squelches my fantasies of exposing our family secrets, the voice that makes me shrink in fear of what my father would do to me if I did. But today, I am weary from lack of sleep and wiped out from the poisoning of the prunes. Maybe it's this and the fact that I am not thinking clearly that gives me courage and makes me decide I *am* going to tell my teacher as soon as I get inside.

Sister Joan stands in the classroom doorway, saying good morning to each student as they pass through. I put myself at the end of the line, reciting over and over in my mind what I am going to say to her, my heart pounding so loudly in my chest, I can barely think.

"Good morning, Diane," she says.

I say good morning back, and as I pause there, all of the words are suddenly gone from my mind. My tongue feels bloated and heavy in my mouth. I hear the clock on the wall inside the classroom ticking away the few seconds I have left to speak.

"Guess what?" I look up at the nun's face, and before she has a chance to answer, I blurt it out. "My father made us eat bad prunes last night, and we all puked."

The words ring loud in my ears, as though I screamed them. I look quickly around, certain my father will burst through the front door, pound up the stairs, and drag me away. Sister Joan stiffens, her brow furrowed in confusion.

"What did you just say?" She peers at me closely now.

"My father gave us bad prunes last night," I rush on, heart slamming against my ribcage.

There is no turning back now. "They were in a dented can. They were supposed to be for the pigs, but he made us eat them, and we puked all night long." I am breathless, blubbering on as I watch her reaction.

Sister Joan is thinking—I can tell by the way she purses her lips and folds her arms across her chest. I feel hopeful and jumpy all at once. She reaches down and takes my chin in her hand, tilting it up until she is looking directly into my eyes.

"Now, Diane," she says softly. "I doubt your father made you eat bad prunes."

I feel panic inside of me. *She doesn't believe me. This isn't going like I thought it would. How can I make her believe me?* I plow forward.

"Yes, he did. He *did*." My voice grows high and pleading. "The prunes smelled rotten. Kathy said so. He made us eat them anyway. Matt and Michael and me are the only ones who came to school today. Everybody else is home sick from puking all night."

But Sister Joan frowns down at me. "Please stop saying that word," she scolds, tightening her grip on my chin. "And your father did *not* make you sick. Your family most likely has the flu that is going around right now."

She has lost her patience with me, her tone harsh and dismissive. But I am alive with anxiety, shaking my head with tears in my eyes.

"No, we don't have the flu," I plead. "He *did* give us bad prunes. Ask Matt . . ."

But doubt is written all over Sister Joan's face. She grows cross—tells me to stop now, to get into the classroom and take my seat. Before I can say anything further, she places her hand flat on my back and pushes me firmly through the doorway. Disappointment descends like boulders falling from the sky, crushing me beneath the weight. I sit in defeat, my stomach weeping with hurt. I fight against it, clenching my teeth and my stomach muscles. Hurt doesn't get me anywhere. Hurt just hurts. Anger, I decide, is better. Anger is power. And just like that—*poof*—it is as though a match has been struck.

Fuck you, my mind screams at the nun. *I trusted you. I thought you would help. Fuck you.* I stare defiantly at Sister Joan as she begins class, hoping she will look into my eyes. Hoping she will feel the heat and see the fury there, like flames licking the blue right off my eyeballs.

———

I wake to the rumble of a car slowly rolling down the road. The night is quiet, the air thick with the perfumed fragrance of budding lilac bushes. Even the crickets are silent. I climb down from my bunk bed and go to the bedroom window, which faces the sloping front yard and the ditch that runs alongside the road at the bottom of the hill. I am in the house's new addition, in the bedroom I share only with Mary. I'm not yet used to this space, the privacy, and the miracle of an actual door.

The approaching headlights illuminate the outline of a fat-bodied moth clinging to the screen on the open window. Gravel crunches as the car halts at the end of the driveway. Lights snap off, and the engine shuts down, plunging everything back into hushed darkness. I am not afraid. I know what this is. Strangers often appear in the dead of night: city people who think farms are the perfect place to abandon their unwanted pets.

I peer out as the passenger door opens, and in the dim dome light, I watch a woman plant her foot on the ground while keeping the rest of her body safely in the vehicle. City people. Probably never seen a black sky or heard a cow moo in the vast darkness.

"Go on," the woman whispers, pulling meowing kittens from a box—three, maybe four of them. She places them on the ground, urging them away from the car, then draws her leg back in. Before her door is fully closed, the man behind the wheel restarts the engine, turns the lights back on, and shifts into gear. Red taillights move quickly down the road, leaving the world quiet again, except for the meowing.

I listen to their cries, hoping the kittens find their way to the barns and join the other cats, hoping they don't wander off to get lost in the miles of fields or swooped upon by an owl looking for an easy meal. I climb back into bed, fretting about the new arrivals.

In the morning I am relieved to find them, three orange-and-white puffballs nestled together on a hay bale in the Front

Barn. I kneel to stroke their downy heads and scratch their ears. I go all soft inside as they stretch and purr beneath my touch, tiny tails straight in the air.

"Let's get you some milk," I coo, carrying the trio to the Big Barn where Lizzy is on her stool, milking Bossie. Lizzy and I look after the barn cats, sneaking milk to them when my father is not around, and keeping them out of his way when he is. It is difficult work, especially now, after the spring explosion of new litters. My father believes our cats' only purpose is to eat mice, and things turn ugly when he catches them anywhere near the milk pail.

"Aren't they so cute?" I ask, full of pride as though they were my own.

Lizzy nods in agreement, reaching out to pet the kitten closest to her. She squirts warm milk into the dish I hold beneath the cow, and they crowd around, nudging each other, meowing in unison. They lap the frothy liquid—milk mustaches on limp whiskers. When they finish, the kittens wobble drunkenly back to Lizzy, meowing and rubbing their tiny bodies against her leg. I watch with a swelled heart, wondering if this is how mothers are supposed to feel about their children.

"Now, don't get in the cow's way, or you'll get stepped on," Lizzy scolds them in her sweet singsong voice, steering the kittens gently away from Bossie's hooves.

She looks up at me and her tone gets serious. "It's time to find a safe place for them before Dad gets home from work."

My father is back to working the night shift, and we know he will be home any minute. He cannot tolerate cats in the barn. If he isn't already in a bad mood when he slides the barn door open, he gets into one very quickly when he sees cats swarming around Lizzy, trying to climb into the milk pail for a taste. Keeping them out of here is tough; between the holes in the walls and the door always opening and closing, they easily slip inside without being seen. We plug holes and deliver dishes of milk to new mothers in their nests, but still, they manage to get in. It's like a game of follow-the-leader. Kittens on unsure feet tumble in a line behind their mothers at milking time. I carry them back to their nests, pleading with the mothers, but they keep coming back.

"I know," I respond. "I'll go build a place for them in the upper barn. It'll only take me a few minutes."

I head up the steps and through the doorway to the main floor, hurriedly arranging hay bales into an enclosure. Lizzy shouts my name and I return to find that a mother cat and her four kittens have joined the new arrivals. The mother is on her hind legs at the milk pail and the kittens are everywhere—tumbling in the straw, marching single-file along the wall.

"Dad just got home," she whispers, her face grave and pale as we lock eyes.

Lizzy nudges the mother cat away and I spring into action, grabbing up the nearest kitten, and the next. I am reaching for a third when the barn door rolls open, and there is my father in the doorway.

"What's going on here?" His eyes scan the room.

"Nothing," I say, holding the animals close. "I'm just getting the kittens out of the way."

He spies the empty milk bowl and frowns. "I thought I told you I don't want you feeding milk to the cats." His eyes fall hard on me.

"We just gave them a little," Lizzy peeks out from behind the cow, trying to keep the mood light.

My father is unmoved with his heavy brow and square shoulders. The mother cat climbs back up the milk pail, and before Lizzy can react, my father crosses the room in two strides, snatches the cat by her neck, and throws her against the wall.

"I told you I don't want these damn cats drinking from the bucket, didn't I?" he snarls.

"I'm getting them out," I say, scooping up the third kitten, one of the new arrivals. I turn toward the steps, hoping to get them to the safety of the upper barn before anything else happens.

"Put them down," my father shouts.

I freeze mid-stride, heart thumping as I hold the squirming kittens protectively to my chest.

"Please let me put them up here," I beg. "I've built them a pen. They won't be able to get out of it." I rush on. "I promise they won't get in the way again." I start up the steps, hopeful.

"I said put them down, *now*." He steps to the barn door. "Michael, get over here," he bellows into the barnyard.

And now I am trembling, well aware of why he called Michael. I bend and set the kittens gently on the floor, touching them, stroking them, and trying to keep them near me. One escapes, trotting back toward the milk pail as Michael arrives, out of breath from running, worry painted on his face.

"Get rid of these cats," my father snaps at him. Just then, the escaped kitten crosses in front of him and my father swings his boot and kicks it hard across the room. The tiny thing yelps, landing with a thud on the floor.

Michael relaxes when he realizes he is not here to be punished. He grins, his eyes magnified and spooky behind his thick lenses. He likes this stuff. He and my father, they have that in common. My father is the tree and Michael is the apple.

Lizzy rises, blubbering. "Please don't do this," she pleads. "They're just kittens."

My father ignores her; his eyes are on Michael, who is in the corner removing The Club from its nook. The kittens are everywhere. I cannot keep them contained. My brother raises the heavy stick in the air, bringing it down with a crack on one of the little heads. Blood flows from the skull, tongue clamped tight between shattered teeth on a broken jaw. I moan and back away, feeling like I might vomit. I stumble and fall hard on the steps.

My father has a term for what he has summoned Michael to do. He calls it Clubbing Cats. And now Michael is moving swiftly across the room like a bolt of lightning against the sky, swinging The Club over and over, delivering fatal blows to the other kittens: one, two, three, four. The sound of the wood against bone, against the concrete floor, echoes off the walls. I watch a pair of beautiful pale blue eyes explode out of their sockets from the impact. One of the eyes flies across the room and out of sight. The other stretches out in front of the kitten on a single thin string, like a loose button on a shirt. All of this happens within seconds, but I see it in slow motion, every single brutal action in perfect detail.

Michael descends on the mother cat, still dazed on the floor. He misses his aim, striking her on the hindquarters with another sound of breaking bones. The cat yowls, eyes wide in fear. She pulls herself across the floor on her front legs, dragging her broken body behind, trying to get away. This is worse than the kittens. Maybe because she is so much bigger than they are. Maybe because she is a mother.

I turn away, feeling dizzy as my brother raises The Club one more time. The barn falls silent again except for the sound of my brother's labored breathing. He wipes the blood off The Club on the straw in the gutter behind Bossie.

"Good. Now get them out of here," my father says with a satisfied nod at Michael, who beams as though he has just done something to be proud of. If I had the guts, if I weren't so afraid, I would fly at him—at both of them—with fingernails and teeth.

Lizzy is sobbing and my father tells her to finish her milking, then orders me to get back to work. I rise on shaky legs, like I am in quicksand: heavy feet, muddy mind. Trembling hands wipe hot tears from my face. I return to my chores, numb from the sights and sounds, angry at myself for not protecting the helpless creatures.

You can't even protect yourself, a voice in my head mocks. *What makes you think you could protect them?* The truth of this presses on me like a heavy weight—the crushing burden of hopelessness.

I watch Michael cross the barnyard, balancing a flat shovel of tiny carcasses that he tosses into the fully-loaded manure spreader. He returns to the barn then reappears with the mother cat, held upside down by the tail, and casually swings her in with the others.

Later, I stand beside the manure spreader, staring at the bodies strewn carelessly atop the stinking mess of piss and shit and straw. If not for the dried blood and the broken faces, if not for the swarming flies flitting in and out of nostrils, I could almost convince myself that the cat and the kittens are asleep here, just dozing in the lazy afternoon sunlight.

I wait for an ear to flicker, a tail to twitch.

1970

A Slip of the Scalpel

It feels like revenge when my father falls off the pump house roof. Mom intercepts us on the porch after school on Friday to give us the news that he slipped while repairing the roof. He is now flat on his back in bed and in a foul mood.

We tiptoe to our rooms to change into our work clothes. Mary and I giggle behind our bedroom door, agreeing that we hope he is in a lot of pain.

My father shouts for us all to come see him before we go out for chores. We line up along his bedroom wall, watching him grimace and *ow, ow, ow* when he turns his head to look at us.

"Did your mother tell you I fell off the pump house roof? And that I had to crawl all the way to the house because she didn't come when I was calling for help?"

Mom comes in with a bottle of aspirin and a glass of water, shaking her head. "I already told you, Richard. The washing machine was running, and the kids were crying. I didn't hear you."

We all stand silent as he scowls.

"I want the Front Barn shoveled out tonight after chores. Just because I'm not out there, doesn't mean you're on vacation."

Out in the Big Barn, Kathy lets out an exaggerated sigh. "Boo-hoo. The big baby."

She gets down on her hands and knees, crawling slowly across the floor. "*Rooose*," she whines in mockery. "*Rooose*, help me."

We crowd around her, clapping and snorting. She gets off the floor and says she thought it was funny when none of us asked him if he was okay. We are pleased that she is pleased.

Michael grins. "I wish I had a pair of steel-toed boots so I could kick him in the ass all the way to the house." We laugh as he mimics my father swinging his boot.

"Or he broke his neck and was paralyzed," I chime in.

"No, no," Kathy says. "Then he would still be around. I wish he had just died."

The weekend unfolds under the dark cloud of my father's mood. He can't get comfortable, says the mattress is too soft. Matt and Michael drag a sheet of plywood through the house and into the bedroom; Kathy and Lizzy help my mother lift the mattress so the boys can shimmy the plywood under it while my father snaps at them to hurry up, he can't stand up much longer. I watch all of this from the kitchen table, my stomach churning with angst. I am no less afraid of my father when he's lying on his back than I am when he is mobile. He settles back in bed with more *ow, ows*, ordering Mom to fix his pillows and adjust his legs.

"Goddammit, Rose, be careful." He growls endless demands: *Get me a glass of milk. Put a blanket on me. Get another pillow under my head.* My egg salad sandwich gets stuck in my throat as I watch my mother rush around in a frenzy.

My father continues his tirade all the next day. By suppertime, Mom is so spent and grouchy that she puts Kathy and Lizzy in charge of baths.

"And I don't want any nonsense from any of you," Mom warns.

Michael and I are on dishes duty, so we stay in the kitchen while the others head off. I'm thinking about my bath, hating the idea of being in the tub with Luke, but I'm afraid to make my plea to my mother tonight. She is at the stove, muttering and scrubbing the top, *shh, shh*ing me every time I accidentally clink dishes together.

Without my father insisting on *Jackie Gleason*, my siblings have the television on low volume and tuned to *Adam-12*. I join them after finishing the dishes, ear cocked toward the bathroom, fretting about the dreaded moment when I have to shed my clothing in front of my brother.

"Luke and Mary, you're next," Kathy shouts. I turn to see her standing in the utility room with Mark on her hip, wrapped in a towel. She fakes exasperation at the surprise on my face. "Well, duh, you're almost ten," she says. "You *should* be taking your own baths."

And just like that, I am gifted my first bit of privacy. Not by my mother but by my hero.

Later, after Luke and Mary exit the bathroom, I undress beside the tub, acutely aware of my nakedness. The tub feels enormous as I submerge completely, arms stretched overhead, toes pointed. My skin squeaks along the bottom of the tub as I move around, savoring the first few moments, suds up to my chin. Alone. Finally.

But as the water grows cold and bubbles disappear, I sit up and look across the expanse of the tub, listening to my siblings in the other room, laughing together at *Get Smart*. I realize I haven't laughed in here or played. I don't have a bubble beard. I hate to admit this, but I miss Luke and Mary. I miss our play. Bathing alone, it turns out, is boring.

I wish Sister Joan had never mentioned the Sins of the Flesh, had never pointed out that our bodies are changing and that we *must* keep them hidden from others. Something is gone—I am vaguely aware of this—something I know I will never get back. I slide down beneath the water one more time, watching the bubbles rise from my lips as I slowly exhale.

———————

My father returns to work and to hours of standing on the factory floor, which worsens his pain and his mood. He works the swing shift now, leaving the house each day at two in the afternoon and returning home long after we've gone to bed. It's my favorite shift because on school days I only see him in the morning.

He has trouble sleeping when he gets home, though, and by morning he is in a wild fury. He shadows us as we go about our chores, shaking a handful of Bayer aspirin into his mouth from a bottle that jingles in his front pocket, chewing them dry. He holds his back with one hand, shouting at me not to put so much bedding down for the calves, can't I see we're going to run out of straw at this rate? And why don't I have the grain in the trough yet? I better stop my dillydallying and get to it.

He moves stiffly, as though a board is nailed to his back, cursing, and threatening me. But he is unable to bend and strike me, and I see frustration growing in his eyes with each passing day. I am grateful to escape the thrashing but fearful he is tallying offenses and will dump his rage on me all at once when his back is better.

———————

"Hold the end of that board," my father shouts over the roaring saw. I do so, taking care to keep it steady on the sawhorses as he buzzes the blade through, the smell of sawdust rising in the chilly fall air.

His back is well enough to resume weekend projects, and today, Lizzy, Michael, and I are helping him renovate the tiny, ancient portable shed that, until now sat abandoned in a far field. We are building rabbit coops for the breeding operation Luke started several months ago when Bob O'Donnell gifted us a pair of white rabbits.

When the first litter arrived, Luke nailed makeshift cages together in a corner of the Front Barn to house the babies. In no time, those bunnies were old enough to breed, and soon Luke was having trouble keeping up with the cage-making. Seeing the value in my brother's efforts, my father butchered some of the rabbits, adding their meat to our regular diet.

We are making good progress on the coop. Two rows of plywood shelves are complete, divided into cozy spaces that run the length of the back wall. Not that there is anything cozy about rabbit breeding. Michael and I were there the first time Luke mated his rabbits, the doe fighting against his heavily gloved hand as he lowered her into the buck's cage. She silently quivered as the buck mounted to rapidly and forcefully hump her. I had never seen such a thing and stood in horror, wondering if *this* is how it is with humans, too, my mind going back to the day I peered under the curtain and saw my parents' naked bodies. Watching the rabbits, I imagined my father on top of my mother, jamming his penis into her while she silently quivered beneath him. Michael stood next to me, nose pressed against the mesh wire of the rabbit cage, and whispered, "*Coool.*"

Luke had grinned, hands deep in his pockets, tickled that he had impressed his big brother. He grew more confident when, a month later, the female delivered a litter of eight bunnies, tiny, pink, hairless things with eyes tightly shut. The operation took off from there, with more and more litters coming one after the other.

That success had made my brother smug. But the smugness disappeared one day when he found an entire litter slaughtered, some of the babies half-eaten. I was there with him, sick to my stomach at the bloody carnage. A buck had broken into the cage overnight. Feeling threatened, the doe did (as Luke learned too late) what rabbits do. She killed her young and mauled the buck in retaliation, shredding his ears and biting off part of his foot. I cried while Luke retrieved the little bodies, the doe watching from the deep recesses of her cage, blinking but not moving. Since then, Luke has been more attentive, working harder to make sturdier cages. But still, there are mornings when he finds rabbits hopping freely about the barn.

The late-afternoon temperatures have dropped, and the October wind kicks up, pushing colder air through the shed's glassless windows. Wet snowflakes fall from the darkening sky, land on the grass, and turn instantly to ice. When I'm not holding a board as I work on our weekend project, I rub my hands together to keep them warm.

Michael is on his knees outside the new coop, stapling chicken wire to the wooden frames that will be the cage doors. Snow accumulates on his back and shoulders. He pauses for a minute to pull the flaps down on his red trapper hat.

My father has me fetch his drill bits and tells Lizzy to plug the drill in. I hold the small box open, and he chooses the one he will use to attach the hinges to the doors. My sister and I smile at each other, excited to see this project coming together, especially with our father in a decent mood. He inserts the little key to fit the bit into the drill, turns it to tighten the chuck, and then hands the tiny key to Lizzy for safekeeping. She looks down, realizing she doesn't have any pockets, and gives the key to me. I tuck it safely into my jacket pocket, under my hand-kerchief. Michael brings in a stack of doors, and Lizzy holds them in place while my father screws on the hinges. I busy myself across the room sweeping up wood shavings, careful not to raise too much dust.

Outside, the mail truck rumbles to a halt at the far end of the driveway, and my father tells me to get the mail. I zip up my thin jacket, tying the hood tightly under my chin, and make my way across the lawn and down the long driveway. The snowflakes have turned from flurries to sleet that now soaks through my jacket and splatters my glasses, blurring my vision. I use my handkerchief to wipe the lenses, head bent against the icy wetness.

Inside the mailbox are a few bills for my father, a colorful grocery store flyer from IGA, and a large, pink envelope addressed to Miss Diane Vonglis. My face lights up when I recognize Gramma Vonglis's long, sloppy cursive. She remembered. My birthday is in three days, and Gramma remembered. All the way from California. I tuck the other mail under my arm and open the envelope, oblivious now to the cold and sleet. A cartoon clown holding red and yellow balloons smiles out from the card. The caption, written in bold, black letters, reads, *WOW! YOU'RE 10!*

Inside, the card is filled with Gramma's scrawled message. She asks how I am and if I am still writing and drawing pictures. I have been sending her artwork and essays from school. She tells me she really liked the last story I sent and says she shared it with her friends. And she tells me she misses me and loves me. Her words spread warmth inside of me.

I read the card again, so wrapped up in Gramma's words that I am unaware of the commotion erupting back at the rabbit coop. When I finally notice the shouting, I lift my head from the card, squinting through my splattered glasses into the distance. My father is leaning out the doorway, waving his hands in the air at Lizzy.

"Well, then go and get it," he screams. I watch in confusion as Lizzy runs, not toward the house but down the driveway toward me. The warmth inside of me fades and my stomach tightens as my sister gets closer. But still, I cannot figure out where she is going.

"Quick," she breathes. "Give me that key I gave you to hold."

And then it all clicks, and my stomach loosens with the relief that this is not going to be a crisis after all. The project has stopped because my father does not have the drill key to change the bit and he's impatient, that's all. It's here in my pocket—an easy fix. Lizzy extends her hand toward me, palm up, ready for me to drop the key in so she can tear back to the coop with it. I reach into my pocket for the little tool, feeling around the balled-up handkerchief, but it's not there. I frown and check the other pocket. Nothing there either.

"Hurry!" Lizzy is frantic.

I pull the handkerchief out and shake it, feeling around inside again, searching for a possible hole in the lining where it may have dropped out. Still nothing.

"Where is it?" Lizzy demands. "Where is the key?"

I turn my pockets inside out, reaching down to my pants pockets to check them as my heart starts thumping inside my chest. I throw the mail back into the box and drop trembling to my knees, searching the snow at my feet. I raise my eyes to Lizzy, who stands over me open-mouthed.

The key is gone.

We retrace my steps, slowly moving side by side up the driveway, our eyes on the ground. My father screams again, and now Michael stumbles toward us.

Oh my God, oh my God, oh my God, my mind screams. *I've lost the key to the drill.*

"What's taking you so long?" Michael shouts. "Gimme the key."

I start crying when I tell him I've lost it.

"Goddammit, Elizabeth, where is that key?" my father bellows from the coop. "Bring me that key *now.*"

"Keep looking," Lizzy whispers. "I'll go tell him we're trying to find it."

I watch her go, thankful my sister is taking some of the responsibility. Lizzy has a different relationship with my father than the rest of us do. He treats her better, doesn't blow up at her like he does the rest of us, and hits her less. I don't understand why. Maybe it's because Lizzy doesn't have a defiant bone in her body and she works very hard to please our father, always saying yes, always agreeing with him. Or maybe it's because Lizzy is the prettiest of us girls and looks the most like him with her black hair and high cheekbones. Whatever it is, I hope she will be able to defuse his anger.

"How the hell could you lose the drill key?" Michael mutters, which doesn't help at all. I heave panicked breaths, pulling at my pockets again and again, hoping the key will appear. We check every inch of ground, kicking at the earth as we do in case it is hidden beneath the fresh snow. My father paces as we approach, red-faced, hands clenched into fists at his sides.

"Where is that key? Where is it?" His eyes are wild, teeth bared. I cower at his feet, words I am terrified to say stuck in my throat.

"I don't know," I finally whisper. "I lost it."

In this moment, the earth grows deadly quiet around me. It feels as though the sky has been sealed off with a thick coat of gray paint, trapping me beneath it. My father swings his steel-toed boot, kicking me with a force that lifts me into the air. I land on my stomach, the wind knocked out of me. And then things begin moving in slow motion, the way they always do when a beating is coming.

He grabs one of the old boards we'd torn off the shed, raises it high above his head, and shakes it at Lizzy. My sister shrinks back, shielding her head with her arms. He growls animal-like but does not hit her. Instead, he turns and stomps over to where I am still on the ground, trying to get air back into my lungs.

"Get up," he hisses, and when I do, he swings the board, striking me on the back of my leg at the knee. The board breaks on impact, the blow knocking me to the ground. It feels like a knife tore through my knee. He throws the board aside and picks up a fresh two-by-four.

"Go find that key," he screams, delivering another burning blow, this time to my rear end. I yelp, crawling frantically across the snowy grass, trying to get away from him.

"*Find it! Find it!*" His rage swirls, tornado-like, and I shriek as snot runs freely from my nose. Three more blows land.

"Don't you *dare* get up until you find that key!" he roars.

Hysterical, I race across the hard ground on all fours, trembling fingers searching every blade of icy grass as I go. He follows me, the board coming down six, seven, eight times.

"Find that key! Find it right now!"

My hands grow numb from the cold, and the knees on my pants become soggy and stained. Something is wrong with my right leg. I can't feel it, and I drag it behind me, whimpering and panting, the panic inside of me pounding in my ears. I move up and down invisible lines, seeking a lost key I know I will not find.

After the beating, after combing the entire side yard on my hands and knees, after my father swallows another handful of aspirin, I am released to do my evening chores. When I stand up, I realize I cannot fully straighten my right leg or put weight on it. I limp to the barn, and once there, I turn to discover blood soaking through my pants at the knee.

In our bedroom that night, Mary shakes her head and cries like she always does when we show each other our injuries. The welts and bruises on my bottom burn and throb, but I'm more concerned about the leg with the long, deep gash running vertically across the back of my knee. Each time I try straightening my leg, the wound breaks open, and oozes fresh blood.

"I think there must have been a nail in the board," Mary says. Her eyes are wet with compassion, and I wonder, not for the first time, what we would do if we didn't have each other in these moments. Having our own room has made us much closer. After lights out each night, we share our fantasies about all the ways our father might die, whispering them from the safety of this room with a door on it.

Mary helps me into the top bunk, and I ask her to hand me the card from Gramma. I turn onto my side to take the pressure off my injured leg and numb bottom, and I read the card again.

WOW! YOU'RE 10!

Hot tears blur my vision, and as Mary turns off the light, a huge, drenching sadness washes over me.

In the morning, I am still unable to straighten my leg. I hop on my left foot to get around as I go about my chores. With each step, the wound throbs, and I have to stop often to catch my breath and gather strength.

When my father goes into town to buy a replacement drill key, I limp into the house to show my mother the injury. There is an unspoken rule against talking openly about our beatings, so it's often hard to know how much she realizes about what goes on outside and what she pretends not to know. She is in the utility room stuffing wet clothing into the dryer, so I wait quietly in the doorway until she closes the lid. Then I ask if she can look at my leg.

"Why? What's wrong with it?" Her voice is tired; her face is tired. She bends, loading more laundry into the washing machine.

"I can't straighten it all the way," I say.

"Well, lift your pant leg, so I can have a look." She sighs. The lighting is poor here, and she pauses from her work to squint at my leg.

"You've already got Mercurochrome on it. I don't know what else we can do." She turns her back, scooping Sears detergent into the machine from the fifty-pound box nearby.

"No, I don't," I tell her. "I haven't put anything on it yet."

A look of surprise flashes on her face. "Okay. Let's go to the kitchen where I can get a better look." She closes the lid on the washing machine and wipes her hands on her apron. In the kitchen, she has me take my pants off and lie face-down on the table. She lifts my right leg closer to her face, and I cry out in pain when she touches the wound.

"You've got a string or something in here," she says.

I turn my head to look, and sure enough, there is a long, thick thread embedded in the wound. Like a wick in soft, red wax. It must have come off my pajamas last night. Mom leaves the table, rummages in a drawer, and returns with a pair of tweezers.

"Hold still now," she says as she lifts my leg again. And then she stabs at the wound, trying to remove the thread. It feels like she's shoving glass into my leg or tearing off a not-yet-ready scab. I jump around on the table, yelping with each poke while she grumbles, "Hold still, hold still."

She finally gets it out and then gently sets my leg down. She is quiet for a long time.

"How did this happen again?" Her tone has softened.

"He hit me with a board yesterday. I think there was a nail in it."

She retrieves the Mercurochrome (her favorite remedy), releases several stinging drops into the still-bloody gash, and then covers it with a large Band-Aid. She doesn't kiss it to make it feel better like the mom in the television commercial, nor does she remark on the bruises that extend far beyond the elastic of my underpants.

"Keep an eye on it," she says as she helps me down from the table and back into my pants.

I am being dismissed. I can tell she wants to get back to her day, but I don't feel like we're done here. This is the worst physical injury I have suffered at my father's hands, and I am scared—really scared. I want my mother to be scared, too, or at least worried for me. I want her to ask more questions about what goes on outside, to show some interest and concern for me. Mostly, I want her to do something. I want her to protect me. I want to break the silence of this taboo topic and start a dialogue about my father's abuse.

But years of conditioning *against* speaking out have left me unable to find the words, so I stand there in the kitchen tangled up in bitter emotions, not toward him but toward her. I feel frustrated that she ignores the abuse, angry that she never steps in, and fearful that she might be afraid, too. My worst feeling is sadness at the possibility that maybe she just doesn't care.

"You probably ought to get back outside before your father gets home." Mom moves to the sink, opens the cupboard above it, and replaces the little bottle of medicine.

I am still unable to straighten my leg when I return to school on Monday, and I struggle to get on and off the bus. Lizzy helps by carrying the birthday cupcakes Mom made, chocolate with light green frosting and sprinkles. Today, I am ten years old. I'm excited about celebrating my birthday at school and sharing the treats with my classmates. I get in line with the other fifth graders, and Lizzy hands me the shallow box, asking if I can manage from here. I say "yes," and she disappears to her own line.

My newest friend, Patty, comes down the sidewalk, waving and yelling "Happy Birthday!" I smile and blush as other kids turn my way with their greetings. Patty lives in town, so she walks to school. She has a big Italian nose and Cher hair that hangs all the way down her back. She steps in line behind me, her brown eyes on the cardboard box. She peers in at the brightly colored cupcakes, licking her lips.

The bell rings and the line shuffles slowly forward. We are packed in so tightly that Patty doesn't notice my limp until we get to the stairs. I grab the railing for support, balancing the box of cupcakes on the palm of my other hand. Sweat breaks out on my forehead as I struggle up the flight, hopping on my good foot while I drag my injured leg behind me.

"Why are you limping?" Patty's brow creases as she watches me take the steps one at a time.

Her look of concern is so genuine that it catches me by surprise. The muscles in my chest loosen and my heart quivers in response. Tears tickle at the corners of my eyes. I open my mouth and the truth nearly slips out. I want to tell her so badly. I want to share my burden with my friend, but I know my father will beat me much worse if I do. So I tell Patty a lie—a lie about tripping and falling down our basement stairs over the weekend.

I watch with a mixture of sorrow and relief as her face relaxes and the concern in her eyes fades, taking along with it this missed opportunity to divulge what has really happened to me.

"Geez, clumsy. You're lucky you didn't break your neck." She laughs then, and I laugh too, happy to put the lie—and the truth—behind me as we move to safer topics.

"Here, let me carry the cupcakes for you." She takes the box, unburdening me in a way I had not intended. As the bell stops ringing, we file inside, one ten-year-old girl carrying a box of cupcakes, the other her family secret.

———

Fifth grade feels much different from previous school years, or maybe I just notice more of what's going on around me—like how the boys tease the girls, and instead of getting annoyed like they used to, some of the girls giggle and seem to enjoy it. I don't know yet how I feel about boys; I am just trying to figure out how to blend in. My father can switch from his Home Face and personality to his Church Face with ease, but for me, it is getting more and more difficult to leave the fearful farm girl behind every time I step on the bus. Who am I when I'm not under my father's thumb? And where do I put the terror and anger from home when I am at school? This struggle causes me to constantly reinvent myself.

On the playground, I mimic Barb's tomboyish ways. When we're out of earshot of the mothers who supervise us at recess, we are foul-mouthed and tough-acting, and we invite ourselves to play football with the boys on the asphalt behind the rectory. They are skeptical at first, but when we convince them to give us a chance, we play as hard as they do, crashing into members of the opposite team and yelling "fuck you" at every opportunity. Soon, Barb and I are picked ahead of some of the weaker boys, and we join the other boys in calling them wimps and sissies.

Back in the classroom, I tone down the language, but I remain feral and mean. I add biting sarcasm to the way I treat my less aggressive classmates. It all makes me feel powerful and in control, and when I am voted class clown, I believe it is an affirmation that I really *do* fit in.

But I don't just want to be mean and tough. I want to be smart, too, like Julie, and I am happy when she asks Patty and me if we want to play Nancy Drew. Julie has all the books at home, and I've been borrowing them from her like crazy. I agree to participate as long as I can be Bess. Patty is George, and Julie, naturally, is the ace detective.

We wander the schoolyard during lunch hour, looking for crimes and clues. When the mothers on recess duty aren't looking, we sneak over the fence to the post office next door and study the Most Wanted posters. Later, we convince ourselves that we see one of those men on the sidewalk in front of our school. We huddle, wondering aloud if we should tell the teachers, call the police, or keep quiet. Julie says we should keep quiet until we make an absolutely positive ID of the man.

I savor these moments at school—the adventures, the fun, and the brief refuge school provides from my other life. My real life. But that's the problem. School is just a temporary place. Most of the time when I'm here, I feel like I am half awake, drifting in a dream. Nothing about it feels exactly real, not the kind of real that home is. And maybe that's why I am constantly changing my persona as I struggle with the nagging sense that I don't quite belong here. I carry so many secrets around that sometimes it feels like they are alive, and I have to fight to keep them hidden. I worry endlessly that one or more of them will pop out of a pocket, a lunch bag, or my mouth at any time.

My mother disappears. I don't know where she went, or why, or if she is coming back. I sit in the kitchen at suppertime with my hands under my bottom, fretting about her being gone. It is unsettling not having her here; the room seems unbalanced and half-empty even with eleven of us crammed around the table. I notice a lot of whispering between my father and Kathy, which deepens my worry. Sometimes I think I am going to suffocate on the secrets in this house.

We learn about my mother's whereabouts in bits and pieces. She is in the hospital, but not to have a baby this time. Her doctor found a tumor in a gland in her neck and believes it might be cancer—Hodgkin's disease, to be specific. The gland needs to be removed. "She'll be home in three days," my father assures us.

Kathy makes grilled Velveeta cheese sandwiches for supper, and while they taste fine, she doesn't hover above us in that familiar way my mother does.

Three days pass, and when Mom is still gone, I wait expectantly for more information, clues about what is happening to her, and an explanation for the delay. The tension around the table is different from the usual tension. This is quieter and feels less threatening because my father shares it rather than causes it. Finally, he speaks about what happened, about how there had been what he calls "an accident" in the operating room. His face is pale, and his voice is soft when he tells us how we nearly lost our mother.

"The doctor's scalpel slipped and sliced too deep, cutting into your mother's jugular vein. She almost bled to death on the operating table."

The news comes as a gut punch, and with it, fear. Fear that my mother is going to die. Fear that it will then be just us and him. I have never considered my mother's mortality before, and I wait for him to reassure us she is not going to die, that she is going to return home.

"Don't worry," Kathy jumps in, responding to our troubled faces. Our sister, not our father, provides the comfort we need. "She's going to be okay."

"We'll say an additional prayer for her," my father adds.

Later, I lie in bed fretting about what will become of us if my mother dies and we are left completely to my father. Will he be capable of expressing grief? Will he soften at her loss, or will he be compelled to drive us even harder because of it?

The tumor turns out to be benign. The cancer scare is just that: a scare. But the results of the slipped scalpel are very real. When my mother finally comes home, she is pale and has a thick, white gauze bandage around her neck. She looks fragile and older, and when she turns her head, it is with a slow, deliberate motion that makes her wince. She isn't allowed to lift anything heavy because of the deep incision that will take weeks to heal. Kathy stops doing outside chores to take over the cooking, the cleaning, and the caregiving for my little brothers.

For a while after Mom's scare, we live in harmony as a family. My siblings and I stand at the arm of the chair where she spends a lot of time during her recovery. We ask how she is doing, whether she needs anything. My father doesn't place any demands on her as she moves slowly around the house, nor does he raise his voice—or anything else—against me and my siblings. We eat a lot of sandwiches for supper as Kathy takes the helm of running the household, an adult in her own right at fifteen.

It is strange to undress for bed at night and not feel the burn of welts on my bottom or the tenderness of fresh bruises. I wonder if I am being selfish in thinking how good Mom's cancer scare has been for me. And as she suffers the daily pain of her slow recovery, I wonder what I would do if I could go back and change the course of this event. Would I prevent that scalpel from slipping and save my mother from all the pain she endures as a result of the doctor's mistake? Or would I let it happen, welcoming the reprieve from my father's attacks at my mother's expense?

1971

Who Scratched the H?

My father orders us—jacketless, bootless—outside. We shiver in our shirtsleeves as he points to a jagged crack running horizontally across the windowpane on the porch door. He wants to know *who* broke it, and he wants to know *now*.

Here we go again, I think. The door is ancient and prone to swinging wildly in high winds; it probably blew shut and broke the glass. But I dare not suggest this, worried he will take it as defiance, so I remain silent with the rest of my siblings. My father calls out to each of us, his breath visible in the chilly spring air.

"Michael? Diane? Any idea?" he asks. We both shrug and shake our heads.

"Luke? Mary? Simon?" All three deny knowledge as well.

"What about you?" He turns to my three oldest siblings. All of them shake their heads, too. We wait as he paces in front of us, arms crossed, red-faced and fuming.

"Well, I guess you'll all just stand out here until you figure out who did it."

Back in the house he goes, to the supper Mom was about to put on the table when he stormed in. His outbursts are getting crazier and more frequent. We rub our upper arms for warmth, blowing heat into cupped hands, whispering how ridiculous this is. We all know that no one broke the window, but we also know one of us will have to confess. My father's need to find fault, place blame, and dole out punishment is an obsession, and until he gets satisfaction on all three fronts, no one is safe, and everyone is afraid. This fear has created a new group dynamic of pressuring the youngest to take the blame. Simon is six. The rest of us circle around him, working together to coax him into admitting he broke the window.

"Come on—you're little. You can say it was an accident, that the door just blew shut."

"Yeah, say you tried to grab the handle, but it was too late."

"I'll bet he won't even hit you."

We agree with one another, knowing full well none of this is true. Simon stands in the circle, looking worried, and tells us he doesn't *want* to say he did it. But we are relentless, begging him, pressuring him, threatening him. That's what we are now, vultures closing in on the easiest prey. When Simon starts blubbering, Lizzy finally comes to his defense. That's Lizzy, always the first to crack, always the nice one.

"Oh, let's leave him alone." She puts her arm around Simon, and we fall silent again, returning to the task of fighting the cold as the sun sets, leaving a frigid, cloudless sky behind.

My father reappears, wiping his mouth on the sleeve of his flannel shirt.

"Well?" he asks. "Have you figured it out yet?" We shake our heads, teeth chattering.

"You can stay out here all night for all I care. Nobody's coming in this house until I hear who broke that window." He turns and goes back inside.

We shiver and stamp our feet as another hour goes by. The sky blackens, and an icy wind moves viciously through our thin clothing. Finally, Michael lets out a loud sigh.

"All right," he says. "No sense in everybody suffering. I'll say I did it."

I look at Michael, wondering at his offer to sacrifice himself for the rest of us. He has done this before—taking the blame for things he claims he did not do. Why does he do this, given how mean he can be and how mean we are to him?

"But I ain't taking the blame after this." He looks from one of us to the next, his eyes flat behind the lenses of his glasses. "One of you assholes needs to say you did it next time."

Matt sprints over to the kitchen window and raps on it. He doesn't want Michael to change his mind.

"Tell Dad we know who did it," he shouts when Mom appears.

My father comes back out and stands on the porch step above us. When he asks who did it, Michael steps forward. Matt is sent for The Club, and when he returns, my father tells the rest of us to go into the house for supper. We rush toward the porch, the warmth of the house, and the mouthwatering scent of burned pork chops. None of us thank Michael for taking the blame. I avert my eyes as I leave the sidewalk, pretending I don't see my brother bending forward to hold his ankles or my father's arm high in the air. I pretend I don't hear the swoop of The Club, the *crack* at contact, and the first *oomph* from Michael.

This is who I've become. Who we've become.

In my room later, I turn on my radio. Melanie is singing her Top Forty hit "Lay Down (Candles in the Rain)." It's a song of peace and protest against the Vietnam War. In my mind, it's a protest song against my father's war, his aggression. I sit on the floor and sing along.

I like that Melanie goes by her first name only. It feels powerful and independent, and I wonder if she, too, wanted to rid herself of her father by dropping her surname.

Along with books, music has become my distraction from life—my comfort, my escape. Here, in the privacy of my bedroom, I learn the words to every song that plays on the radio, the melodies and lyrics providing me with a nightly salvation, even if it's only a temporary reprieve from reality. As Melanie's voice rises along with the chorus behind her, I feel their collective strength here with me in my room. I sing along, harnessing the power of their rebellion and taking it as my own. I feel included in the protest, and that makes me feel somehow safer.

––––––––––

My father is back to working the day shift at Gleason's and back to grumbling at the supper table about how he is wasting his time working there. He complains about his aching back and standing all day on the concrete floor. We hear about that aching back all the time now. He threatens to quit soon, muttering about how he should be here, running the farm, not cooped up in some factory. To prove his point, he goes outside after we finish chores to "check our work." He calls it his Nightly Inspection. We never know what he will find during these Nightly Inspections. It is something new every night—we didn't spread enough straw for the cows' bedding, or we spread too much straw; the hay rack is only half full; the barn floor isn't swept properly; the pigs still seem hungry; a pitchfork is broken; a hinge on the chicken coop door is coming loose. The list is endless.

Last week, he marched us to the cow pasture behind the Big Barn, side-stepping broken boards and old tractor tires tangled up in the tall grasses, so he could have us stand in a circle around a small pile of shit, nearly hidden from view by a clump of weeds. It clearly wasn't from a cow, but it could have been a coyote or one of the bigger barn cats. But no, my father was sure a human had left this pile, and he wanted to know which one of us it was. When no one confessed, The Club came out.

These are the offenses we face as a result of our father's growing frustration with being trapped inside a factory all day.

And as his rages spin further and further out of control, so do the nonsensical charges that are hard to tie to any real logic.

Tonight, he waits until supper is over, and we've bowed our heads to thank God for this and that. As we head off to do our homework, he heads out for the Nightly Inspection. Distracted and anxious in my room, I struggle to finish my math assignment. And then I hear it, his heavy footsteps on the porch, the slamming of the utility room door. He screams our names as he roars into the house: "Kathy, Matt, Lizzy, Michael, and the rest of you. Get outside. *Now.*"

The nightly chaos begins as my sisters and I rush from our bedrooms, and the boys pound down the stairs from theirs. We shake and fumble into our shoes as my father shoves us one at a time through the doorway, yelling, "Get out there. Get out there. Get out there." I hurry out the door with the others, tripping down the steps at Lizzy's heels.

"Get over here," he snarls, stalking off across the lawn. We follow, crossing the driveway and continuing to the side yard. My shoes squeak on the damp grass. Dusk settles, chilly on my shoulders.

My father stops beside the old Farmall H tractor, which is parked under the willow tree. Since we got our new tractor, the H has looked more like a relic than a legitimate piece of farm equipment. The paint has faded further, and large patches of rust cover most of its frame. A coffee can is still wired around the muffler on top. And yet it is at the old H tractor that my father now points.

"I want to know who did it," he says. "I want to know who scratched the H."

The tight fear inside of me loosens. I have nothing to do with tractors. I don't know how to drive them, and the nearest I ever get is to hitch a wagon to them. One of my brothers must have crashed the tractor into a fence or scraped it alongside one of the hay wagons by accident. It would be easy to do—the old thing is always lurching forward on its own because of its faulty clutch. I've watched Michael up on that metal seat, struggling to control the tractor while yanking on the steering wheel as though it were the reins of a wild horse. There have been a lot of near misses. I look the tractor over but don't see any visible damage. I turn to the others, who seem equally baffled.

"Don't give me those faces," my father growls. "One of you did it, and I want to know who."

Matt moves to the side of the tractor, hands and eyes running up and down the body, searching for a fresh gash or a new dent.

"It's here," my father snaps, pulling a flashlight from his back pocket and pointing the beam at a spot just below the steering wheel. In the bright halo of light, I see a jagged white vertical line. It is about the length of my index finger, faint, and paper thin. Michael, with his bad eyes, has to lean in for a closer look. When he does, my father shoves hard against his chest, knocking him to the ground.

"Don't act like you didn't know about this," he hisses down at my brother, now sprawled in the dirt.

I know I should feel bad for Michael, but the idea that my father might already think *he* did it sends a small ripple of relief through me. If Michael can be blamed, I can be spared.

"Maybe the key accidentally scratched it when one of us was starting the tractor up." Matt shrugs. "See how it's right there next to the ignition keyhole?"

"Yeah, or a boot buckle could have rubbed up against it and scratched it. There isn't a whole lot of legroom there," Kathy adds.

I am grateful to both of them for their voices and their bravery, especially Kathy, who speaks her mind more and more these days. She is in tenth grade now, giving her a two-year edge over my father's entire education, something I believe bothers him.

"No." My father shakes his head at her. "No. Someone did this on purpose."

We shrug and look at one another, then at the tractor, then back at him. He starts pacing, his large hands balling into fists. The cold air gathers thick around us. No one moves except Michael, who quietly gets up off the ground. I lock eyes with him. *Will he be the scapegoat for this?* Michael glares back at me with hard eyes.

My father stops pacing and places his hands on his hips. His jaw is set in that scary way. Face red. Eyes narrowed.

"I am going to ask you one more time." He looks from one of us to the next. "I want to know *who* did this, and I want to know *now.*"

No one moves or breathes.

"No one wants to confess, huh? Fine, then." He points to Luke. "Go get The Club."

And then he is shouting for us to get in a line. My legs turn to jelly, and Mary whimpers at my side. We shake and blubber as Luke races across the darkening barnyard to the Big Barn where The Club waits, as always, in the nook just inside the door.

The next day at school, I can hardly sit on my chair. My bottom throbs, and my upper legs tingle with numbness. Mrs. Nichols, my sixth-grade teacher, drones on about the Romans or the Greeks or the Egyptians. I'm not sure which—I feel as though my ears are stuffed with cotton, garbling her words. Not that I care, not that ancient history has any relevance to my life.

Back home that evening, my father is still whipped up about the scratch on the H. I imagine he stewed about it all day at work, standing on the concrete floor with that aching back. After chores, he lines us up beside the tractor again, screaming that one of us did this, and by God, he is going to find out who it was. The Club comes out again, and with each blow, he hollers, "Was it you? Tell me! Did you do this? Did you scratch the H?"

Later, in my bedroom, Lynn Anderson is on the radio reminding someone that she never promised them a rose garden. Mary and I compare bruises: white welts from today, and the mottled purple-and-blue patches underneath from yesterday. My rear end feels like it is on fire, and my homework goes untouched. We turn off the light and whisper in the dark about how much we hate him. I lay on my right side to take the pressure off my injuries, my head leaning over the side of the top bunk bed. Mary wonders aloud if we could put rat poison in his cereal.

At my desk the next day, I tuck my leg under my body to shift the weight off my burning bottom. My mind is numb. I am in school, here but not really here, watching the second hand sweep across the face of the clock on the wall. In two hours, I will be home again, plucked from this place of short reprieve and dropped once again into my real life. Until she calls my name, Mrs. Nichols's voice is just a hum in the background of my thoughts. I blush and ask if she'll repeat the question.

"I asked you, Miss Vonglis, in what region did all of this take place?"

I have no idea what "this" refers to, and I stare at her exasperated face, feeling the blush deepen on my own.

"Pay attention, young lady." Mrs. Nichols taps the map on the wall with her pointer stick. "You're daydreaming back there, and if it continues, I'm going to have to move you to the front of the room."

She's right, of course. I am daydreaming, and my grades have suffered as a result. I used to be a straight A student, but this year I dropped to Bs, and, to my horror, I got a C in history. My first C ever. I don't know how to turn around my academic decline. I'm not even sure if I care. As life at home worsens, I slip further and further out of this pretend world of school, consumed throughout the day by images of what my father has done to me and dread of what might be waiting each evening.

So while Mrs. Nichols's threat to move me to the front of the room is humiliating, it is also meaningless. For all I care, she can nail my desk to the fucking blackboard. It won't change a thing.

The mystery of Who Scratched the H is still unresolved, and by the fourth night, my father has us in the line before supper. I bend again, worn and sore, ground down by defeat. Michael is next, and when he puts his arm behind himself to block the blow, I hear a sharp *pop*, like a rifle shot, as The Club connects with bone instead of meat. He lets out a high-pitched yowl and my father strikes him again, screaming for him to keep his goddamn arm out of the way. I understand why Michael did this. I am often tempted to put my hand back there to protect my rear end from the assault. It is a reflex that's difficult to control.

After each of us has taken our blows, my father yells at us to get inside and wash up for supper. We cry and limp, and Mom scurries around the kitchen telling us to sit before the food gets cold. Michael holds his elbow protectively against his body. We bow our heads and fold our hands, waiting in silence for my father to lead us in our evening prayers.

Bless us oh Lord, and these Thy gifts, which we are about to receive from Thy bounty, through Christ our Lord, Amen.

In the morning, Michael's elbow is swollen to twice its normal size, with dark bruising settling in. His fingers tingle and he can't straighten his arm all the way. He waits until after chores, and after my father has left for work, before showing it to my mother. They stand under the light at the kitchen sink while the rest of us gobble our cereal. Mom bites her bottom lip, and Michael winces as she pokes his tender skin. There is no talk about how this happened. She tells him to stay home today, she'll put ice on the elbow and keep an eye on it. To the rest of us, she says, "Hurry and finish up your breakfast or you'll miss the bus."

In my classroom, I count down the hours until the weekend. I wonder how Michael is doing, if Mom let him watch cartoons all day, and what kind of mood my father will be in when he gets home from work. I wonder how I am going to survive a fifth night beside the H.

After school, we see that Michael's elbow is still swollen. The bruise is wider now and blue-black in color. Mom says she called Doc Collins, and he wants my brother to go for X-rays tomorrow. *Again?* I think. Michael was in for X-rays a few months ago, also for a possible broken bone because my father had beaten him so badly he could barely walk. He had suffered for almost a week before my parents finally took him for X-rays. Later, Michael told us our father had done all the talking, lying to the doctor about a heavy barn door that had fallen on his son. Apparently, my mother sat quietly by. The X-rays came back negative for a fracture, and the doctor concluded the bone was bruised.

Mom looks worried, and I wonder if she is worried about Michael or worried about how my father will react to the news of needing more X-rays. A hot flash of anger at her rushes through me. *Useless*, I want to scream at her. *You are fucking useless.*

When my father arrives home from work, he goes into the house but does not come back out. Later, in the kitchen, he sits rigidly in his chair with a scowl on his face. Michael is beside him in The Chair, looking pale and cradling his arm. Mom flits back and forth from the stove to the table. The room is quiet, but the deepest silence is between the three of them. I'm dying to know what happened when my father learned that Mom called Doc Collins. Did he ask what story she told the doctor? (And what story *did* she tell him?) Did he argue with her about the need for X-rays? Was he angry at Michael? Did he blame my brother for putting his arm back there? Did my mother defend Michael at all?

We eat and pray, and afterward, it's my turn to do dishes. I dry while Luke washes. Walter Cronkite keeps my father company in the living room. When the dishes are done, I tiptoe past his chair, then down the hallway to my bedroom. There,

Mary and I try concentrating on our homework while we wait to be called for the nightly lineup. But the television stays on, and when my father hasn't moved from his chair by nine o'clock, I gratefully climb into bed.

In the morning, Michael gets in the truck between my parents, and they head off to Westfall Medical Center in Honeoye Falls for X-rays. Since it's the weekend, and Kathy is left in charge, we talk openly in the safety of our fatherless kitchen. What story will he tell them this time? Will the doctor bother to ask Michael what happened, and if so, will he be brave enough to speak up? Will Mom remain silent like last time?

"Well, you know the bastard already has a story cooked up." Kathy snorts. "He'll turn on the charm with that dumbass grin of his, and the stupid doctors will believe every word." She fills Mark's cereal bowl, pouring milk on top and adding two heaping tablespoons of sugar. We nod and murmur, certain she is correct. Even Doc Collins never gets to the truth when we're brought into his office with lesser injuries.

"Maybe they'll be suspicious and give Michael a complete physical since he was just there a few months ago," Kathy continues. "All they need is to see his butt, and *then* they'll be asking questions."

After breakfast, Kathy says we have a few hours and asks if we want to listen to her records. We carry kitchen chairs to the living room, chattering excitedly while Kathy lugs her record player out from her bedroom and places it on top of the television console. She retrieves her records—45s lined up in a gold wire rack with round wooden handles. My sister has them numbered one to fifty, listed by song and band in her neat cursive, on a sheet of paper she keeps folded in the rack. We aren't allowed to touch the records, but she passes the paper around, and we each get to pick a song. We listen to "Midnight Confessions" by the Grass Roots and "Mama Told Me Not to Come" by Three Dog Night. I pick "While My Guitar Gently Weeps" by the Beatles.

Lizzy chooses Herman's Hermits, and we all sing along in our best British accents about what a lovely daughter Mrs. Brown has. Even Matt, usually reserved, adds his deep voice.

For just a second, my mind wanders as I wonder what is happening over at Westfall Medical Center. I picture the doctor returning to the small patient room with Michael's latest set of X-rays. Is the bone bruised or broken this time? Does it matter? I imagine the doctor nodding as he scratches my father's lies into the chart.

I pull myself back to the living room, to the here and now. My concerns about what is happening at Westfall and whether or not the saga of who scratched the H will continue can wait. Kathy puts the needle down on the record Mary asked for, "Red Rubber Ball." This song always lifts my spirits; the hope that the worst is behind me and that things will be better tomorrow. Lizzy, Mary, and I are side by side, swinging our legs in unison, a wide smile on my face. Across from us, Matt taps the beat on his knees, and Luke snaps his fingers. Simon, Joey, and Mark run in circles around the chairs, giggling and poking one another in the ribs. No one shouts at them to be quiet. No one tells them to settle down. Kathy leans against the television in her hip-hugger jeans and wide black belt. Her eyes are soft on us, like a loving mother.

A breeze blows through the torn sheer curtains on the picture window facing the street, carrying the scent of wet wood, dead leaves, and cow shit. The boys run faster and faster as the song builds. My sisters and I lean closer to one another, our faces lifted, and our mouths open, joining voices for a loud, final refrain.

1972

Cow Heaven

As promised, my father quits his paying job at Gleason's in the spring to become a full-time farmer. He is home all the time with his temper, his moods, and his demands. Without the moments of reprieve we used to have when he was at work, we all take on rigid postures, poised to jump, defend, or just get the hell out of his way. At supper one evening, he announces he has a new idea.

"A real money-maker." He smiles as he cuts meat away from the edge of a steak bone. "We're going to start a veal operation."

He nods as though agreeing with himself as he pushes a slice of meat between his teeth. "That's where the *real* money is these days." He makes another cut and, between mouthfuls of food, lays out the details of his plan. Forty calves at a time. A new state-of-the-art barn with giant fans built into the walls to circulate the air, an automated gutter system that carries the manure out of the barn with the flick of a switch. His elbows are on the table now, shoulders stiff and square. We aren't responding with the enthusiasm he wants, but what is there to be excited about? More work? More animals? More stress?

Jackass, I think. *You said the same thing about raising beef years ago. That was supposed to be our money-maker.* I look around our kitchen: same battered stove, same chipped dishes, same shitty curtains.

My parents take out a big loan from the bank in town, and we start building the calf barn when school lets out for the summer. A cement truck arrives, pouring thirty tons of concrete out of a long, foldable trough into the hole we dug for the building's floor. My father rakes the heavy, wet mixture into place while Michael and I get on our knees on either end of the two-by-four that spans the width of the area. Back and forth, back and forth we push the board—he on one side, me on the other—slowly screeding the concrete to perfect flatness. My arms strain and ache under the weight of the cement against the board. It is also a game of beat the clock because the cement must all be in place before it hardens.

Harvest time slows the project as we head into the fields to gather oats and wheat, then hay and straw. We live a sunup to sundown working existence.

Kathy isn't around much anymore since she got a full-time job at a restaurant in town. She is saving money for college, a decision she made without so much as a word of encouragement from either of my parents. At first, my father argued against the idea of her taking the job, saying he needed her here on the farm, but when Kathy suggested she could pay rent in exchange for being gone, he agreed. I feel more vulnerable without her here, more alone. I envy my big sister's newfound freedom, and even though it's not fair, part of me is angry at her for abandoning the rest of us.

But my admiration for my sister is greater than these fleeting moments of anger. Kathy has made the Vietnam War—the one I used to laugh about with Barb—very real for me now. I listen to her strong opinions against the war, opinions mirrored on television by bearded, shaggy-headed men and women in flowy, flowered blouses marching in the streets. I like the feel of the movement: the signs the protesters carry, the shouting, the rebellion. Kathy sews a peace sign onto the sleeve of her jacket and stitches the word "peace" into the denim of her bell-bottoms. I ask her about the new silver bracelet on her wrist.

"It's called a POW/MIA bracelet," she says as I run my fingertips over the words stamped into the metal band. "There's one for every soldier captured or reported missing." She continues. "That's the name of my soldier, and the date he was last seen." Kathy taps the bracelet. "We're wearing these bracelets, so people don't forget how many of our guys in this stupid war have been captured or are missing."

Kathy buys a bracelet for Lizzy, too. Lizzy cleans a teacher's house on Saturdays, so she has money to pay Kathy back. When I ask if she will get me a bracelet, Kathy says sorry, she has to save all of her money for college.

At night, while the others are in the living room watching TV, Kathy comes home from work with the daily newspaper. Lizzy and I crowd around the kitchen table with her as she opens to the pages that list the soldiers who have been killed, captured, or reported as missing in action. The columns of names are in small print and often cover two entire pages. Lizzy hovers over the list of soldiers killed in action, twisting the bracelet on her wrist, and whispering, "Please don't let my guy be here, please don't let him be here."

Each night, I hold my breath as we gather together, Kathy unfolding the paper and running her index finger down the columns of names. I have watched my sister slipping slowly away from us, gone from the farm most of the time, taking tiny steps toward independence. She bought an old Ford Falcon from a man at church and put a black bumper sticker with an upside-down smiley face on it. *POWs never have a nice day*, it reads. I sense she has one foot out the door, so I savor being a part of this daily ceremony—the opening of the newspaper, the scanning of names, the bracelets. These are the things that keep my big sister close to me.

And then the day comes when Kathy's index finger stops at a name. I turn to Lizzy, whose face is crumpling, her lips quivering. "No, no," she whispers as tears drop from her eyes. She backs away from the table with her hand clamped over her bracelet, as though hiding her soldier's name will somehow erase it from the newspaper. Lizzy turns and bolts from the kitchen, through the living room, and down the hall to her bedroom.

I look at Kathy, who holds her own bracelet protectively to her chest. She is also teary-eyed. "This fucking war," she whispers under her breath.

We finish the calf barn just as school starts in the fall. I stand inside and have to admit that it's pretty fancy. The fans in the walls are enormous and make a deafening whir when turned on. The barn is long and narrow with bright white walls *(new! clean!)* and fluorescent lighting. My father says there wasn't enough money in the loan to cover the automatic gutters, so we will have to shovel the manure by hand for now.

Our food supply has dwindled since my father quit his job and there is no money coming in. When the cereal runs out, Mom puts a piece of bread in the bottom of each of our bowls, covering it with milk and a heap of sugar. I love sugar but hate the texture of the soggy bread. When I ask Mom if I can have the bread on the side, she says "too late" and puts the bowl in front of me.

School lunches have changed, too. We have gone from bologna and Velveeta cheese sandwiches to just Velveeta sandwiches, and then to bread with Miracle Whip slathered thinly inside. I eat my sandwich before anyone notices what is (and is not) inside.

On Sundays, we go to church without our collection envelopes. Mom used to give us each a dime for the collection, but now she says there's no money. The church usher looks surprised when he extends the long-handled collection basket across our pews and none of us drops an envelope in. Even Mom doesn't open her purse anymore, and I watch her turn crimson, looking down at her folded hands as the basket stops at her and then moves on.

The calves arrive, newborns still rickety on furry, spindly legs. Each gets a black leather collar with a silver ring that clips to chains along the wall—chains barely long enough to allow them to lie down without choking. I feel sorry for them with their giant eyes and their pink noses, all lined up like prisoners, twenty on each side of the building.

The barn is not the only high-tech part of this operation. The calves are on a specific liquid-only diet, made up of water and a carefully measured amount of powdered formula. My father puts me, now thirteen, and Luke, who just turned twelve, in charge of the calves. He works with us the first few days, mixing the opaque concoction into also-new galvanized buckets. We feed the calves one at a time. I know there is a lot riding on this calf operation, and I worry about all the details as my father hovers between us, making sure we do everything right.

We do everything exactly as instructed, yet when winter arrives, we enter the barn one morning to find two of the calves coughing and sneezing. My father sticks a thermometer up their rectums, cursing as their temperatures rise, and thick, green mucus begins flowing from their nostrils. Willy Thompson arrives at my father's request. He points his soggy cigar at the fans and says we didn't install them properly. Air is being sucked into the barn, but none is going out. Willy lifts a tail, shaking his head as yellow stuff drips from the calf's anus.

"Scours. Means you've got infection." Willy is not his smiling, laughing self today. My father listens, face grim, arms folded across his chest, as Willy suggests changing formulas.

We reinstall the fans and switch formulas, but the calves don't get better. They become lethargic and don't want to eat. I hold a bucket beneath a nose, petting the curly black fur, begging the sick animal to drink as it shivers and hunches its back, bleating like a sheep as putrid feces pours from behind. Within days, they are both too weak to stand. Meat shrinks from bones, ribs protrude. My father blames Luke and me and kicks us with that steel-toed boot.

"So help me God, you better not let any others get sick," he threatens.

In response, I get angry at the calves, cursing *them* when my father isn't around. I lift a frail body off the floor by its bony hips, screaming at it to stand up. *Just fucking stand up.* It teeters for a moment before its legs fold in on themselves and it slumps back to the ground. I fight the urge to kick it.

The next morning the calf is dead, splayed stiff-legged in the straw, its pink tongue hanging out of its open mouth. Flies flit on and off eyeballs that stare straight up at the ceiling. I have seen death many times before, but there is something about this emaciated calf lying dead in its own waste that breaks me. Watching it suffer and wither away each day, innocent and trusting, while I showed it no compassion or tenderness. *What is wrong with me?* I kneel in the soggy straw, sobbing and shooing flies as I stroke the soft, curly fur on its forehead. I can't be sure if I am crying for it or for me.

"*Oooh*, shit." Luke enters the barn and crouches beside me. "Dad's not gonna like hearing this."

We stare at the dead animal in silence, neither of us wanting to be the one to wake our father with the news. Luke goes to find Matt, who arrives with a rope over his shoulder and a heavy sigh when he sees the calf. He ties the rope around its back legs and drags the animal across the floor, up and over the doorstep, *bump*, *bump*, and out into the muddy snow.

As expected, my father lashes out viciously, kicking us around the barn, which smells of piss, shit, and foul milk. He has taken out a giant loan for this operation, he yells. It must not fail. But the second sick calf dies two days later, and three more are coughing with runny noses. I get off the school bus each afternoon fretting about what is waiting for me and Luke. Another dead calf? Another beating from my father?

The calves, the calves. My father is obsessed with them. He takes their temperatures, checks the fans and formulas again and again, and rants endlessly about them during supper. My mother moves about the kitchen wordlessly, lips pressed tightly together as he bubbles and boils at the head of the table.

The calves reach ten weeks of age, halfway to slaughter time, but the three sick ones are now down on the ground. My father has us chain them together at the far end of the barn, hoping to keep them away from the healthy ones. They die, and two more are down. Each day starts with fresh anxiety. I whisper, "please don't be dead, please don't be dead" as I open the barn door, switch on the lights, and scan the room. My heart sinks when I find a dead calf sprawled on the floor with its protruding ribs, stiff legs, and lifeless, staring eyeballs.

But it isn't the animals I feel sorry for anymore, it's me and my siblings because we all share in the punishment that follows each death. Every lost calf stokes my father's fury, and we suffer his wrath every moment of every hour of every day.

"Another one." I shake my head when I find Matt in the dark morning barnyard. We have a routine now for the dead calves. Matt ties the back legs together and drags it up the hill of the back field while Luke or I follow along with a flashlight. Today is my turn. I train the beam of the flashlight at the ground in front of Matt as he leads the funeral procession. Our boots poke holes into the crust of last night's snowfall as we trudge along, and Matt stops frequently to adjust the rope around his hand or to catch his breath.

"This sucker's heavier than it looks," he says as we ascend the steep hill.

We created a special place up here in the hedgerow for the dead calves. At first, we lined them up—side by side—in ceremonial solemnness. But as more and more died, our senses dulled, our emotions thinned, and we just started tossing them on top of the others. We call this place Cow Heaven, a grisly graveyard of baby calves in various stages of decomposition, legs jutting out at all angles in the tangle of fur-covered bodies. It reminds me of the disturbing Holocaust movie Sister Agatha showed us in fifth grade—footage of a bulldozer pushing a mass of human bodies across the earth. Naked and skeletal, they tumbled along with bony legs and arms that waved as they fell into a long, deep trench.

It's spooky up here in Cow Heaven with the rancid smell of decay from all these dead animals with their thick tongues hanging from open mouths and their black eyes staring at me. But worse than any of that are the opossums. The sound of them scuttling around in the darkness brings goose bumps to my flesh, and I step closer to Matt. We first noticed the opossums a few weeks ago, two adults chewing away at the meat on a calf tail. The sight frightened and sickened me, and when Matt threw stones at them, they ran off into the woods beyond the field. But the beady-eyed creatures didn't stay away. They had found their food source and, as it turned out, a winter home for their family. Matt took the flashlight into the hedgerow for a closer look one day and saw that the opossums had burrowed a hole in a calf's anus and taken up residence inside. By the beam of light, we saw the small faces of baby opossums huddled together inside the animal's eaten-out cavity. Even he, my brave big brother, had jumped back at that sight. As we've returned again and again, the opossums have become more brazen, hissing at us rather than running off.

I swing the flashlight toward the sound now. Three of the scavengers are on top of the pile, tearing flesh off a newly-dead calf. Below them is the one they made into a home. They have eaten through the side of the animal now, exposing a rack of ribs that looks like the bars of a cage. Behind the bars, several pairs of close-set eyes peer out: ugly mothers, ugly children.

"Don't let them 'possums scare you." Matt is bent over, untying the rope from the legs. I feel protected by his words. He packs a snowball and throws it at the trio on top. They barely flinch. He sighs and says, "Let's get this done."

"Ready?" he lifts the calf's front legs. I nod, setting the flashlight on the ground, and grab ahold of the back legs. We lift the animal into the air, and on the count of three, we swing it up and onto the pile. Only then do the opossums scatter.

We head down the hill in silence, me scuffing along in the snow beside Matt. We slow our pace, knowing what awaits us when we get back, and tell our father we have lost another calf. I watch the sky go from black to gray to pewter as we descend.

1973

The Unraveling

My mother closes her eyes and shakes her head each time she hears about another dead calf. Her face goes pink, and with sealed lips, she breathes an audible sigh in and out of her nostrils. Neither she nor my father come right out and say it, but I know our farm is in serious trouble.

The price of wheat, our only cash crop, drops along with livestock values. Envelopes begin arriving in the mail marked *Past Due* and *Second Notice*. They are from the bank that funded the veal project and from Agway, which, until now, has been gracious enough to allow my father to run a tab on all our farm supplies, tools, and seeds for planting. I pull utility bills and mortgage statements from the mailbox and feel like a traitor as I hand them to my mother.

My parents enlist Kathy's help to sort out their finances. My sister has been working double shifts at the restaurant, trying to secure enough money to go to college in the fall. She says she will try to help them figure things out, but she won't lend them any more money. *Any more?* I wonder. *When did she lend them money? And how much?*

My mother looks embarrassed that Kathy has said this out loud, that she has let a secret slip. My father bites on a toothpick and drums his fingers on top of the table as Kathy scrutinizes each bill, adding numbers to the column making its way down the page in her spiral notebook.

———

Two weeks later, all the veal calves are dead. We come home from school to find the last five of them strewn in the snow outside the calf barn. We learn that when my father discovered yet another dead calf this morning, he flew into a rage and stormed to the house to get his rifle. Back in the barn, he put a bullet through the foreheads of each of the four remaining healthy ones and then tossed them all out into a heap. I stare at their tangled legs, gaunt bodies, and vacant faces. A line of blood runs from each perfect bullet hole between the eyes onto the ground. The blood is dry now and has stained the snow a rich burgundy color that reminds me of cherry snow cones.

The shiny new barn, once the pride of our farm, now sits as a giant oblong failure among the broken-down buildings and equipment that surround it. Lights out, fans off, doors shut.

My father is at the head of the supper table, coiled like a snake ready to strike. He doesn't talk about what happened or what will happen next. Except for the before and after prayers, not a word is spoken during the meal. Heightened hysteria hangs in the air, almost tangible, like morning dew. I feel it on my skin and in my throat: electric, alive, and dangerous.

———

I kneel behind the black curtain of the confessional booth, heels touching the wall behind me. In the hushed darkness, Father Farrell clears his throat from his booth on the other side of the wall in front of me. A small window slides open, revealing a heavy mesh screen. It is the only thing now separating us. I can't see him because of the booth's blackness, but he is close enough for me to smell his breath of garlic and sour milk.

Earlier, the nuns and teachers had marched us in lines, two abreast on the sidewalk, here to the church for Confession Day. We come once a month to admit to the sins we have committed. Little sins. Venial sins. It is expected that none of us have or ever will commit a mortal sin, the big ones that send you straight to hell. This little black booth, we are told, is the safe place to unburden ourselves of our sins. And only through the priest, hidden on the other side of the booth, can these sins be heard. Only through the priest, there in the shadows behind the mesh screen, will God hear our pleas for forgiveness. *What sins, I wonder, does my father confess to when he kneels in this booth?*

"You may begin, my child." Father Farrell's chair squeaks as he leans closer to the screen. I recite the expected, memorized response.

"Bless me, Father, for I have sinned. It has been four weeks since my last confession. These are my sins."

I made up my list of sins on the way over here—three sins this time. I switch it around for each confession. Sometimes I only confess to two sins, sometimes as many as four. Never more than that, though. And the irony that I lie about the sins I have committed causes a little jiggle of pleasure to erupt inside of me each time I enter the booth.

"Go ahead," Father Farrell coaxes from the other side of the screen.

"I hit my brother last week. I said a bad word. And I was mean to one of my classmates."

"Are you sorry for these sins?"

"Yes, Father."

"Are you willing to ask God's forgiveness for these sins?"

"Yes, Father."

"And do you vow not to commit them again?"

"Yes, Father."

I wait in the darkness as he calculates my punishment.

"You are to say one rosary, and two Our Fathers for your penance today."

"Yes, Father."

"Now go in peace to love and serve the Lord."

"Yes, Father."

"Amen, child."

"Amen, Father."

I leave the booth, holding the curtain open for Julie, who is behind me in line. Then I scoot into a pew beside my friend Patty, who is on the kneeler with her head bowed, saying her own penance. I wonder how many Hail Marys and Our Fathers and rosaries Father Farrell would assign to the two of us if he knew about the real sins we commit right here in this church.

Patty and I regularly sneak over here during lunch hour to warm up when it's freezing outside. At first, we just sat in the pews. Now we wander around, exploring the places we normally don't get to see—up the creaky, winding stairwell to the choir loft, and then further up to the bell tower, where we sit in the biting wind and look out over the rectory, the convent, and the schoolyard beyond. We smoke cigarettes Patty steals from her mother's purse, then go back downstairs, through the vestibule, up the church's long center aisle, and onto the altar, where I mimic Father Farrell blessing the bread and wine.

In the room behind the altar, we open a closet to find the altar boys' red and white cassocks hanging in a row on wooden hangers. Three of my brothers are altar boys, and I'm secretly jealous of the stuff they get to do. I watch them light candles on the altar with that fancy wooden staff every Sunday and then snuff them out at the end of mass. They bring bowls of water to the priest with a fancy napkin folded over their arm. They get to hold that round gold plate with the handle under our chins as Father Farrell places the host on our tongues during

Communion. It's supposed to be there in case the host falls, but when Michael is the altar boy, he jabs it into my neck as though by accident.

In a second closet, I run my fingers over the silky purple-and-white robes Father Farrell wears on special occasions. We find boxes of tapered ivory candles and that neat thing on the gold chain that sends smoky incense wafting into the air when the priest shakes it. It produces a smell so strong that I've seen old ladies pass out under the cloud of it, the mass coming to a screeching halt as parishioners rush to their sides and wave hymnals in their faces to revive them.

My favorite thing is lighting the Memorial Candles that sit in red glass holders on a three-tiered rack against the wall to the left of the altar. For a quarter, you can light one of these candles, either in memory of someone who died, or with thoughts of a sick person, and it will burn all week. When I was younger, I would plead with my mother to let me light one. I loved the ceremony of it: the plunk of the quarter dropping into the metal box in front of the candles, the strike of a long, wooden match, and then the glow inside the red glass as the wick catches the flame. "No," she would always say. "We don't have money for that."

Patty and I don't need money. We just light the candles—all of them—and then blow them out and relight them. It is every bit as gratifying as I had dreamed. I jiggle the locked box that holds the coins. While the candles burn, we go around touching more things we aren't supposed to touch: statues of weeping saints, and the stone-carved images of the Stations of the Cross hanging in rows along the church walls. We flick holy water from the marble fountain at each other, laughing about what would happen if we added red food coloring to it. Would people think it was some sort of sign from God? A warning? A miracle?

I kneel beside Patty, bowing my own head, pretending I'm saying my penance. But I'm really thinking about what we did here in church yesterday. About how I dropped a match on the floor after lighting a Memorial Candle, and the match rolled so far under the rack that I had to go behind the rack to retrieve it. And when I was back there, I discovered that the lock on the coin box was a fake lock. I found the box completely open in back and loaded with quarters.

"Bingo," I shouted out to Patty, scooping up a handful of them for her to see. We agreed to take only a few each, and with the coins tucked in our uniform pockets, we ran from the church, across the street to the little grocery store there, and bought Hostess pies—cherry for me, apple for her. We bought Ho Hos and Cracker Jacks, stuffing our mouths as we ducked back to the school yard just on time for the after-lunch bell to ring.

Later, behind the safety of my bedroom door, I rolled up my sleeve and licked the inside of my forearm, then pressed a tiny pirate tattoo from the bottom of the Cracker Jacks box to my skin. I added skulls and crossbones, a butterfly, and an alligator, transferring the blue ink from the little squares of paper in a neat row. I smiled with self-satisfaction when I was finished and rolled my sleeve back down. *My father can have his secrets*, I thought. *But I can have mine too.*

The failed calf operation marks a pivotal moment in the unraveling of our lives and deals us a catastrophic financial blow. By summer, my father is desperate for cash and decides to hire me and my siblings out. Matt and Michael get in the front of his truck as Lizzy, Luke, Mary, and I climb in the back. We are headed to the next town over where my father has made a deal for us to harvest another farmer's hay for a fee.

"Don't we have enough of our own work to do?" I mutter as we pass our own unattended hay fields. The air is already sticky with humidity, and I am in a foul mood.

"Yeah but we're getting paid for this," Lizzy replies, as though either of us will see so much as a nickel of the cash.

The farmer has two tractors and several wagons to fill. Matt and Michael will drive the tractors, and the rest of us will work in pairs loading the wagons. My father shakes the other man's hand, tells us he will be back later to get us, and then gets into his truck and drives off. I feel angry and degraded. This farmer is wealthy. He has a welding business, horses in a stable, and a teenage son who runs behind our wagon catching mice as we work. When he gets bored, he wanders off to sit under a tree with his dog in their sprawling yard.

The sun is setting when we climb down from the day's final stacked wagon. I am exhausted and dreading that we still have animals at home waiting to be fed. My father arrives and the farmer presses some bills into his hand, saying my father must be proud of his hard-working kids. My father's peacock feathers briefly appear as he folds the money into his pocket.

My parents leave the house on a hot summer day after lunch, dressed in their Sunday clothing. It is Wednesday, so we know they are not headed to church, but they're evasive about where they *are* going, my father saying only that they have business in town. We speculate about their destination, agreeing that they are probably meeting with the bank about the loan.

The phone rings as we are getting ready to head out for our afternoon chores. Our phone doesn't ring often, and when it does, Mom is usually here to answer it.

"I'll get it." Mary runs excitedly into the kitchen.

My father has a Rule about answering the phone. If the call is for him, you must write a note saying who called, when they called, what they wanted, and their phone number. I wait for Mary as the others head outside, watching her animated face as she listens to the caller and scribbles on a piece of paper.

"That was weird," she says when she hangs up. "It was Father Farrell calling for Dad. He wouldn't say what he wants, just to have him call when he gets home." She glances at the clock. She adds the time at the bottom of the note and then lays the paper in the center of the table.

Later, at supper, Mary asks my father if he saw the note about the phone call.

"What note?" my father puts his fork down slowly.

"I left it on the table," Mary continues. "Father Farrell called while you were gone. He wanted you to call when you got home."

"I didn't see a note." My father looks at my mother, who shrugs. He pushes his plate forward. "Where is the note?" His words are measured.

"I left it right here on the table," Mary persists. "It said, Father Farrell called, and he wanted you to call him when you got home. He gave me his phone number. I wrote it all down."

"She did," I jump in. "I watched her write the note. It was right after lunch."

"Where's the note?" My father is standing now, and I feel the air being sucked out of the room as his face goes from red to purple.

"*Where's* the note? I don't *see* the note." He is screaming now, his hands balled into fists. *"Find the note! Every one of you! Find the note!"*

We jump from our chairs and start running around the house, looking behind the fridge, under the stove, and in the cushions of the couch and chair. I scatter utensils from kitchen drawers onto the counter as he yells *"Find it! Find that note!!!"*

Lizzy opens cupboards behind me, pulling dishes out, searching under plates and inside pots and pans.

"Where is that note!?" My father paces between rooms. *"So help me God, you better find that note!"*

My hands shake as I rummage through the same drawer I just checked, and I watch the mass hysteria grow around me. Lizzy pulls back the curtains while Luke searches the windowsill with his fingers and Michael runs to check the bathroom. I keep one eye on my father, who is dragging a bag of old golf clubs from the porch into the living room, clubs that someone gave us years ago and that have gathered dust in a corner of the porch since then. I am on my knees now, frantically digging through the kitchen garbage pail, and he is pulling a club from the bag.

Joey cowers in a corner as my father approaches him with the golf club. Mary steps in front of our little brother and holds her hands in front of her face as the club comes down with a *crack* on her forearm.

"Where is it!? Where is the note? Find it!"

The golf club hits her again, this time bending on impact. He throws it aside and grabs another from the bag.

"Find it! Goddammit, find that note!"

Mary braces herself against the blows with bent knees as red welts rise on her exposed forearms and dishes crash to the floor from the kitchen, where Luke has climbed to the highest shelf and swept everything off it with one hand. Simon squeezes under the couch for another look and Matt and Michael pull the stove clear away from the wall. Still, we cannot find the note, and the golf clubs come down again and again. As one bends, my father flings it across the room and grabs another. I want to jump in to save my sister, but I'm afraid I'll get hit too. My mother stands behind me, her hands trembling on my shoulders.

"Mom, do something," I yell.

"Richard, please stop." Her voice is weak and unconvincing, and I feel a *whoosh* of anger explode inside of me. I want to scream at her, *Act like a goddamn adult for once. Be a mother and protect us for Christ's sake.* I rip myself from her grip and turn on her.

"Do something! He's going to kill her!"

She finally moves closer to him and shouts, in a much stronger voice, "Richard! Please! Stop!"

Later, in our bedroom, Mary says she doesn't think anything is broken—luckily, the golf clubs were aluminum instead of steel. She holds her swollen arms out to me, describing the pain as mostly numb and tingly. The imprints from the golf clubs are evident in the welts already turning to dark bruises.

The house has settled down around us. Dishes have been put away, furniture moved back into place. Matt sank the bag of golf clubs into the pond.

We get in bed and whisper in the dark, both still shaken.

"Maybe Matt can run him over with the tractor," Mary says from the bottom bunk.

"Maybe Michael will shoot him," I respond.

1974

Escape

I wake to my mother's whispering voice. She is bent over Mary, shaking her awake in the bottom bunk.

"What's going on?" I sit up in the dark, whispering, too, because it is so unusual to have Mom in our room in the middle of the night.

"Your father choked me and threw me on the floor," she whispers back in a shaky voice. "I'm going to sleep in here with you girls."

I watch her shadow glide back to the door and close it completely. Mary is awake now.

"Here, Mom," she says. "You can have my bed. I'll go up and sleep with Diane." She scuttles up the end of the bed, crawling her way across my mattress as I make room for her.

"Thanks, girls." My mother rustles around in Mary's bed but says no more.

Mary cups her hands around my ear. "What's going on?" she whispers.

I turn my head and cup my hands around her ear, repeating what Mom said.

Mary is silent for a moment. "Do you think he'll come in here?" she whispers back.

"I don't know."

"I'm scared." She clasps her hand in mine and I squeeze it in assurance, even as my own heart thumps in my chest.

I lay awake long after Mary falls asleep. Mom is quiet, too, although I cannot be sure if she is asleep or not. Until tonight, I haven't thought much about my mother's personal life or even recognized that she might have one. I have been too engrossed in protecting my own. More and more, she is like a ghost in the house. I don't know what she thinks, if she has any dreams, what her opinions are, or how she feels about her life. I know she loved the Kennedys because she has a tapestry of John and Bobby hanging in the living room and cried buckets when each of them died. But other than that, my mother is like a husk of a person, rarely speaking up on anything and certainly never defending us, which is why I have been so angry at her all these years. She has kept our family life private and, until tonight, has kept her own personal life even more private. But now this.

I think back to that day years ago when I peered under the curtain on the porch and saw my parents' naked bodies, and something loosens in my mind, like a stubborn coin shaken from inside a pants pocket. I had wondered about my father lashing out at my mother in a physical way, and now she has said it out loud. She has made it real.

When I wake in the morning, my first thought is that I had a terrible dream last night, but then I hear Mary stir beside me. The bed below is now empty, blankets thrown aside as though my mother got out in a hurry.

At the breakfast table, neither of my parents acts like anything has happened. It is strange to watch their behaviors knowing what I know. *Is this how it always is? Has this sort of thing been going on for a while?* I watch my mother closely, noticing the distance she keeps between herself and my father.

"Can I talk to you girls?" my mother stands outside our bedroom, her voice hushed as her eyes glance quickly down the hall. I pull the door open as she enters, then close it with a click. A prickle of unease runs up the back of my neck. Mary gives me a questioning look. It is so strange to have her in our bedroom again. Like a foreign object. Mary scoots off her desk chair, and Mom sits with her knees together, feet firmly on the floor, and hands in her lap.

"Go ahead and sit down," she says quietly. I take my place across from her in my own chair. Mary remains at my mother's side. Here we are for a second time, the three of us in the silence of this bedroom.

"I'm thinking of leaving your father." Mom looks at me, not Mary. "I want to know what you think about us leaving."

Her words catch me so off guard that I just stare at her for a moment. Inside, I feel a soft burst of hope explode.

"I think it's a great idea." I lean closer to my mother, so she knows I am on her side. She breathes out a long sigh.

"I can't live like this any longer," she continues. "He just keeps demanding more and more from me. And I'm worried he's going to kill one of you kids."

Hearing my mother say these words out loud gives credence to our dire situation. All this time, we have held family secrets from the world, conditioned by my father through fear and isolation to keep them here on the farm, to remain silent. For her to speak of the secrets, to voice our reality in these weighty words, legitimizes everything I have known to be true.

"Do it, Mom." Mary puts her hand on my mother's arm. Mom smiles at her, then turns back to me. I feel like an adult, helping make an adult decision. It feels both wonderful and terrifying.

"How are you going to tell him?" I ask, worried now for my mother, worried he might kill her if she tries to leave.

Mom contemplates the question, fingers entwined in her lap. "I'm not sure yet, but I wanted to know what you girls thought. I've already talked to the bigger kids. I'll let you know what I decide."

I think I hear a hint of hesitation and wonder what the others said to her. Did they agree we should leave? Did any of them try to talk her out of it? It seems impossible. I lean forward in my seat, desperate to assure her that leaving is the right decision.

"Mom, do it. *Please* do it."

She rises from the chair and tells us to keep this to ourselves, leaving as quietly as she arrived. I turn to Mary, who has a giant grin on her face. Without a word, we clasp our hands and start jumping up and down.

I float through the week, looking for clues from my mother about what she has decided. On Friday, she whispers that she wants to have a meeting with us four oldest kids. With Kathy off to college, I am now one of them, one of the Big Kids. The secrecy is frightening. She gathers us and says she wants to take a vote for who thinks we should leave the farm and who thinks we should stay. She starts with Matt, who says he doesn't really have an opinion, that this is her decision to make. His answer surprises and disappoints me. I had assumed we would all vote to leave. Mom presses him for a *leave* or *stay*, but he remains stubbornly noncommittal.

Michael is next, and his *stay* vote shocks me beyond words. Michael, the one who has expressed the most hatred for my father. The one who has suffered the most abuse at his hands.

"How can you vote to stay?" I am incredulous. Panic rises inside of me at the possibility that I might be the only *leave* vote and we will be stuck on the farm after all. Michael shrugs and mutters something about believing that families are supposed to stay together no matter what.

I turn wide-eyed to Lizzy, who is sitting next to me.

"I vote *leave*," she says. I grab her hand and squeeze it.

My stomach is knotted up as Mom ponders our responses. "Okay," she says. "Let's have a show of hands. Who thinks we should stay?"

Michael's hand goes up.

"Who thinks we should leave?" Lizzy and I raise ours and so does Mom.

"Matt?" He shakes his head, refusing to vote. *Chicken shit,* I think in anger. *Until now, you were one of my heroes. How dare you abandon us at this crucial moment?*

"Looks like we're going to leave," Mom says and warns us not to breathe a word about the meeting. I feel my heart skipping like a stone across the surface of a still lake.

———————

Three nights later, someone bangs on the porch door when we are in the middle of supper, and when Lizzy opens it, a man steps in with an envelope in his hand. I have no idea who he is—no one ever comes to the farm unannounced, especially at this late hour.

"I have serving papers for Richard Vonglis," the man proclaims.

My father rises slowly from the head of the table, his face turning red.

"I'm Richard Vonglis." He snatches the envelope from the man's outstretched hand, and in the blink of an eye, the man is out the door, taking all the air in the room with him. A spooky silence descends. The meal is only half-eaten, but Mom tells us to go to our rooms. Her voice is shaking, and I feel the familiar *tick-ticking* inside of me as I head down the hall to my room with Mary on my heels. Lizzy follows us into our room and closes the door behind her. She leans against it, owl-eyed. In the kitchen, my father shouts at my mother.

"How can you do this to me? You can't take these kids away. How am I supposed to run this farm alone?"

I strain to hear my mother's murmured response, to no avail. Lizzy is pale. Mary is pale. When my father shouts for all of us to get back in the kitchen, we creep out from the safety of our rooms.

"Your mother wants to divorce me. She wants to break up our family." He holds up the papers, his jaw tight, face still red.

"You kids don't want to see that happen, do you?" His tone is more of a threat than a question.

We look at one another and at the floor. No one speaks. Mom inches closer to us.

My father's eyes narrow. He begins to pace. *Here it comes*, I think. *The Club, the beatings, the snuffing out of this idea that we can somehow escape him.*

He looks at the papers again, then glares at my mother. "You want to go? Fine, go. Get the hell out of here."

I look at my mother, heart pounding my ribs. *Is she going to go? Will she abandon us so she can protect herself? Would she really do that? Leave us here with him?* She has not looked away from my father's glare, and I wait in silent agony with the others until she finally speaks.

"Everyone get in the car."

She takes Mark by the shoulders and steers him toward the utility room. She is shaky yet steadfast in a way I've never seen her. We all hurry into our jackets and boots as my father continues his rant.

"Go ahead. Leave. All of you. Get the hell out of my house!"

He stands in the doorway between the living room and the utility room. My hands are trembling so badly I can barely get my boots on. *What if he kills us? What if he changes his mind and just starts killing us?*

I race to the station wagon with the others, certain that in a second, I will feel his heavy hand around my neck, pulling me back, stopping me, stopping all of us from our escape. Mom gets behind the wheel, and before we've even slammed all the doors, she peels down the driveway like she's trying to escape a burning building.

It is pitch black outside and dark in the car except for the glow of the dashboard lights. From the back seat, I watch my mother hunched over the wheel, her jaw set, her face bathed in those lights. Pride swells inside of me. *She's really doing it,* I think. *She's really taking us away from him.*

As we leave the country behind and head into town, a smile settles on my face. I see it reflected in my window each time we pass beneath a streetlight. No one speaks as we pass through town, cross the Genesee River, and continue west.

Mom drops me and my sisters off at Gramma and Grampa Murray's. Nothing feels real to me as Gramma hurries around. She makes up a cot for Lizzy in the upstairs sewing room and points to the spare bedroom across the hall for me and Mary. *What did Mom tell them?* I wonder. *What is Gramma thinking?*

I sleep a fretful sleep, and in the morning, Lizzy wanders in from the sewing room. The three of us wonder aloud what will happen next. Gramma shouts for us to come for breakfast, and we head down the steep staircase to the kitchen where she is dressed in her usual apron, making jelly and butter toast for us. Grampa is off to work, and Gramma still says nothing about why we are here. All she says is that my mother and the boys are down the road at Aunt Ruth's house.

"Hurry and eat your breakfast." She passes the plate of toast. "Your mother called and wants you to come down there when you're done."

We dress and head down the road. It is winter break, so we don't have school, and it seems as though everyone is still asleep in the houses we pass. The stillness is pleasant. I think about what I would be doing right now if we were home. The animals would have been fed hours ago, but what tasks might my father have us doing on this cold morning? Would he already be screaming at us?

When we arrive, Mom is on the phone in the kitchen; Aunt Ruth and Uncle Stan hover nearby. They look nervous, and I wonder how much my mother has told them. My little brothers are scattered on the living room floor, engrossed in cartoons with our cousins. Matt and Michael look out of place, sitting on the couch between two German Shepherds.

Three days pass like this. Each morning, we leave Gramma's house and find my mother huddled at the kitchen table with Aunt Ruth and Uncle Stan, all of them drinking coffee and murmuring in low voices. A folded newspaper sits beside a pad of paper that's filled with my mother's handwriting. *Are they planning our future? Are we going to live like this indefinitely? Is Mom thinking about going back to my father?*

Finally, on the fourth morning, Aunt Ruth shoos her kids into their bedrooms to give us some privacy. Mom gathers me and my siblings in the living room; it's the first time we have been alone together since our escape. I look around: Matt on the couch with his palms up on his lap; Michael perched on the edge of a cushion, jaw set; Luke between them with a worry line creasing his brow. Lizzy and Mary share a chair with the little boys at their feet, all big-eyed and silent. I am on the floor, too, and maybe it's just the angle, but my mother looks taller today as she stands before us. Bigger somehow. I sneak a peek over my shoulder into the kitchen, expecting to see her diminished self still there at the table.

Mom spreads her arms wide and smiles. It's a nervous smile but a smile nonetheless.

"Well, we're really leaving, kids."

She tells us she has found a small house to rent in town; won't it be nice to walk to school with our friends? She also tells us some kind people have offered to donate beds and dressers and other furniture to get us started. She says Mr. O'Donnell found a used washer and dryer and has promised to hook them up as soon as we move in.

I try to keep up with everything she says, trying to absorb the excitement that I hear in her words and see on my siblings' faces. But my mind is still locked on her first sentence: *Well, we're really leaving, kids.*

I have waited so long to hear these words—ever since that fateful night eleven years ago when she sent me outside to call my family in for supper and I opened the barn door to discover who my father really was. I want to savor these words, to hold them on my tongue and in my ears. Sweet tastes, sweet sounds.

She is taking charge of our lives, a voice in my head tells me. *She is taking care of us.* I realize my mother isn't taller or bigger—she has simply stepped out of my father's shadow.

"We're going out to the farm tomorrow," she says. "Your father has agreed to leave for a couple hours so we can get some of our stuff."

The next morning, we pile into the station wagon and drive to Mr. O'Donnell's house to pick up the trucks he is letting us borrow for the day. He has gathered boxes we can use for the move, and he hands Matt and Michael a set of truck keys each. Watching him confer with Mom in his kind, steady voice seems to give her strength, and that brings me comfort. It is decided that Matt will lead in the first truck, followed by Michael in the second truck. The rest of us will follow behind in the station wagon with Mom.

The minute we turn onto our road, my heart beats faster. We pass the few houses situated between snowy fields but don't see any movement. It feels like everyone is hiding, like everyone knows something is about to happen. We crest the final rise in the road, and when our farm comes into view, an involuntary shiver runs through me. Ahead, my brothers turn into the driveway. We follow, the wagon creeping up the driveway to park behind the trucks.

Matt and Michael get out, slam the doors, and head toward the house. The porch is open, but the inside door is locked. Matt shouts this news to us, a surprise given that we've never locked our doors, and says Michael is going around the side to climb in a window. Mom shakes her head and exhales a frustrated sigh.

"Okay, everybody out," she says as she opens her door and motions toward the trucks. "Each of you grab a box. I want to do this as quick as we can."

Luke hops into the back of a truck and hands boxes down to the rest of us. Despite the cold, I feel sweat in my armpits. From the house comes muffled shouting. My brothers are in and I relax a little as I take a box from Luke. But then the shouting is louder. I freeze when I hear my father's voice. I turn toward the house and watch as he backs Matt and Michael off the porch and onto the sidewalk.

"I'll kill the first person who comes through this doorway. I swear I will." He grips a baseball bat in his meaty hands, swinging it high in the air.

Matt takes another step backward at the warning.

"Calm down." Michael holds his ground, raising his hands as though in surrender. "We're just here to get some of our stuff."

I stand beside my mother and the others in the driveway, my heart thumping against my ribs. This was not the plan we had gone over this morning. We'd expected to show up at the farm when we knew my father wouldn't be there, then fill our boxes with clothing, sheets, and pillows. We were going to be in and out before he came back. That had been the plan when we pulled into the empty driveway. But he had tricked us, hiding his truck somewhere, and then ambushed my brothers at the door.

"Rose," he shouts, "get your boys out of here." He holds the bat higher, standing wide-legged in the porch doorway. "I'll kill 'em. I swear. I'll kill 'em."

"Mom, I think we better go," Lizzy whispers. "He'll do it. You know he'll do it."

My mother's face drains of color. "Okay, boys," she calls to my brothers. "Let's go."

Matt and Michael tromp back through the snow, never taking their eyes off my father as they get behind the wheels of the trucks.

"Everybody get back in the car." My mother hurries around to the front of the station wagon and drops into the driver's seat. Lizzy slides into the passenger side. Luke, Mary, and I get in the back seat and the three little ones clamber into the way-back seat.

My mother's hand shakes as she struggles to get the key in the ignition. I want to shout at her to hurry, to get us out of here before he flies off the porch and rushes down the driveway, smashing the car windows with the bat and then dragging us out, one at a time, to beat us to death. Panic traps all my words in my throat. My eyes are on the ignition.

Finally, the engine starts, and my mother backs the wagon quickly down the driveway and onto the road. Only when our procession is far, far up the street do any of us exhale. My heart doesn't slow down until we are safe again in Mr. O'Donnell's kitchen.

We return to the farm two hours later, this time with a police escort, red lights swirling on the roof of the officer's car as we pull in behind him. He leans into my mother's open window.

"Wait here until I tell you it's okay to come in." He heads up the hill toward the porch.

My father reappears with the baseball bat still in his fist.

"Stay back," he yells at the policeman. "Stay back, or I'll kill you, too."

The officer backs away from the porch as Matt and Michael had before him. From a safe distance, he yells orders to my father.

"Sir, you need to step aside and let them through," he says. And, "Yes, your wife *does* have a right to take personal belongings from the house."

"Try to get past me," my father growls, roiling and raging on the top porch step.

The officer comes back to the station wagon. "I'm afraid I'm going to have to call for backup. Just stay put, okay?"

My mother bites her bottom lip and nods.

While we wait, we pelt her with questions. *What's happening? Are you sure another cop is on the way? Should we just leave? What if two police aren't enough? Will they arrest him?*

Mom keeps shaking her head. "I don't know. We'll see. I don't know."

Finally, the second police car speeds down the hill, its lights also flashing. The officer pulls in behind our wagon and gets out with his hand on his pistol. The two policemen talk and then approach Mom's window.

"Wait here," the first officer says again.

They walk in tandem up the hill to the porch. My father had left his post some time ago, disappearing into the house. *To do what? Get his gun? Make his own phone call?*

The police rap loudly on the porch door. When my father opens it, he no longer has the bat in his hand. Even with the car windows rolled down, it is difficult for us to hear what they say. The three of them take turns raising their arms and voices.

"You can go in now." The first officer is back at Mom's window. "He says he won't stop you. But here's the deal. You get one box each. Take only your clothing, nothing else. We're only going to give you ten minutes to get your stuff and get out."

"Ten minutes?" Mom looks stupefied.

"Sorry, ma'am. We don't like domestic scenes. Your husband is pretty upset, and we don't want to push him too far. This is what he's agreed to."

"Come on, kids," she says. We all get out of the car again.

Matt and Michael hand us boxes from the backs of the trucks while Mom issues instructions. "Matt, help Mark with his things. Michael, help Joey with his. All of you, fill your boxes with as many clothes as you can fit. Don't forget underwear and socks."

"And make sure you only take clothes," the officer reminds us again.

We follow him to the porch. I am surprised to see my father standing just inside the utility room doorway. Even though the second officer is right next to him, I feel frighteningly vulnerable at how close he is, certain he will reach out and grab me or swing that steel-toed boot. Every hair on the back of my neck stands up as I brush past him and hurry down the hall to my bedroom.

And then I am standing in front of the closet with Mary, ripping blouses and dresses from hangers that loudly clang together, as though they are voicing the frenzy and the sense of urgency pumping through me. I throw these things into my box along with my church shoes, then drag it to the front of the room. I open dresser drawers to toss in bras, underpants, pajamas, and socks. T-shirts, bell-bottoms, flannel shirts. Mary, also in a state of panic, is on her knees in the closet, near tears as she searches frantically for a second shoe.

"You've got one minute left," the first officer shouts from down the hall.

Mom and Lizzy come out of their rooms with full boxes. When Mom asks if she can please take just a few dishes, the officer snaps at her. "No. I already told you, you can only take your clothes."

In the living room, Mark is crying because he can't pack Sparky, his favorite stuffed animal. I wonder why the officer must be so harsh with my mother and so heartless to a seven-year-old.

"We'll get it later," Mom says to Mark and tells him to follow her out to the car. Matt is right behind her with Mark's box on top of his own. I hear my other brothers pounding down the stairs. The first officer keeps yelling: "Time's up! Let's go! Time's up!"

As I make my way back through the utility room, I hear the second officer speaking softly to my father. "I feel bad for you, sir. I really do. I know this is unfair, and I wish I could do something for you, but unfortunately, this is the law."

I watch him put his hand on my father's shoulder, and it seems that his interest now is in comforting my father rather than defending us. What sob story did my father spin to these officers while we packed our boxes? What lies did he spew as he forced crocodile tears to win them over to his side? I feel a flash of rage toward the policemen, angry that they, like so many before them, are being manipulated. Angry that they believe the lies, apparently forgetting that only a bit ago my father had threatened *their* lives. Two more people letting us down. Two more fooled.

Outside, we load the boxes in the trucks and Mom thanks the police. The second officer pulls his vehicle to the side so we can leave. Mary and I jump in the station wagon's way-back seat as my brothers jostle one another in the middle seat.

"Okay boys, settle down." Mom puts the wagon in reverse and backs out of the driveway. I feel shaky but relieved. We did it. We got our stuff. We're leaving. We really are leaving.

I like the way-back seat. I like how it faces the back window so I can look out at where I've been. I watch my past shrink as we move further and further away from it. From the top of the hill, the barns, the fields, and the house grow smaller. I wish my father were outside so I could watch him get smaller, too. The station wagon takes the bend in the road, moving along until we are shrouded by trees on either side, obscuring my view of the farm. At the stop sign, Mom turns right, leaving Swamp Road behind.

I turn in my seat to gaze out the front window, watching my future rush toward me.

Acknowledgements

First, to my sons, Dean Parnell and Conor Parnell, who read every word of every draft with an enthusiasm that never dimmed. Your thoughtful input, tireless efforts, and sharp, clear insights gave me clarity when I was feeling lost. Thank you for being my biggest cheerleaders. I cannot adequately express my gratitude and love for you.

To my mentor, Willy Bruijns, who took me under her wing throughout the years of writing, and kept me focused on what this story was really about. I am honored by the many hours of smart, honest critiquing you devoted to my project. Your faith in me kept me buoyed throughout the process, and I truly believe this book would not have come to life without your steady guidance.

To the many friends and supporters who offered to read various iterations of my manuscript, thank you doesn't quite cover it. Your candor and suggestions made me a better writer. I'm looking at you: Alyssa Ferrando, Deb LaManna, Sue Foos, Jenny Frost, Kelly Keene, Suzanne Glazos, Meg Orman, Wendy Kennar, Madeline Palaszewski, Donna Elgie, Susan McCreary, Jennifer Ring, Susan Quinones, Margaret Hennessy, Sima Eslambolipour, David Coats, and Dr. Ann Marie Tommey. And to the ladies of the Pismo Beach book club who read an early draft and then invited me for lunch to discuss: Kathy Metcalf, Mary Eister, Mary Miller, Wendy Robinson, Dottie Muckinhaupt, Nancy Gloye, Nina Zanussi, Mardee Whitehouse, Michelle Macey, Meg Dennison, Anita Abshire, and the late Jan Edgerton.

Finally, to the brilliant and talented Brooke Warner of *She Writes Press*, for helping me to separate the wheat from the chaff, and for dreaming up the perfect title for my book. It was a pleasure working with you and your team.

About the Author

Diane Vonglis Parnell grew up on a remote farm in Western New York with nine siblings. Her essay *Blame the Milkman* was a winner in the Fish Publishing short memoir contest, and included in the Fish Anthology 2022. Vonglis Parnell is a Scrabble enthusiast and a lover of progressive rock music. She serves as a CASA (Court Appointed Special Advocate) volunteer for abused children in her community and lives a minimalist's life in a 200-square-foot cottage in San Luis Obispo, California.

Author photo © Kellen Keene

SELECTED TITLES FROM SHE WRITES PRESS

She Writes Press is an independent publishing company founded to serve women writers everywhere. Visit us at www.shewritespress.com.

The Sergeant's Daughter: A Memoir by Teressa Shelton. $16.95, 978-1-63152-721-0. Every night of her childhood life, Teressa's sergeant father brings his military life home, meeting each of his daughters' infractions with extreme punishment for them all. At first cowed by her father's abuse and desperate to believe that maybe, one day, things will change, Teressa ultimately grows into a young woman who understands that if she wants a better life, she'll have to build it for herself—so she does.

The S Word by Paolina Milana. $16.95, 978-1-63152-927-6. An insider's account of growing up with a schizophrenic mother, and the disastrous toll the illness—and her Sicilian Catholic family's code of secrecy—takes upon her young life.

Being Mean: A Memoir of Sexual Abuse and Survival by Patricia Eagle. $16.95, 978-1-63152-519-3. Patricia is thirteen when her sexual relationship with her father, which began at age four, finally ends. As a young woman she dreams of love but it's not until later in life that she's able to find the strength to see what was before unseeable, rise above her shame and depression, and speak the unspeakable to help herself and others.

Serious Little Catholics: A Memoir by Kathy Gereau. $16.95, 978-1-64742-110-6. A hilarious peek into the Catholic school experience through the eyes of Kathy Gereau—who, by learning to laugh at the ridiculous bits of dogma, eventually finds the spiritual message within.

No Rules: A Memoir by Sharon Dukett. $16.95, 978-1-63152-856-9. At sixteen, Sharon leaves home to escape the limited life her Catholic parents have planned for her because she's a girl—and finds herself thrown into the 1970s counterculture, an adult world for which she is unprepared.

Seeing Eye Girl: A Memoir of Madness, Resilience, and Hope by Beverly J. Armento. $16.95, 978-1-64742-391-9. Written for the invisible walking wounded among us who hide their pain behind smile—and for the educators and mentors who sometimes doubt the power of their influence—*Seeing Eye Girl* is an inspiring story of one girl's search for hope in an abusive, dysfunctional home, and of the teachers who empowered her.